CHERRY .

BOOKS BY RITA MAE BROWN

The Hand That Cradles the Rock

Songs to a Handsome Woman

The Plain Brown Rapper

Rubyfruit Jungle

In Her Day

Six of One

Southern Discomfort

Sudden Death

High Hearts

Started from Scratch:
A Different Kind of Writer's Manual

Bingo

Venus Envy

Dolley: A Novel of Dolley Madison
in Love and War

Riding Shotgun

Rita Will: Memoir of a
Literary Rabble-Rouser

Loose Lips

Alma Mater

Animal Magnetism: My Life with
Creatures Great and Small

BOOKS BY RITA MAE BROWN
WITH "SISTER" JANE ARNOLD
IN THE "OUTFOXED" SERIES

Outfoxed

Hotspur

Full Cry

The Hunt Ball

The Hounds and the Fury

The Tell-Tale Horse

BOOKS BY RITA MAE BROWN
WITH SNEAKY PIE BROWN IN THE
"MRS. MURPHY" SERIES

Wish You Were Here

Rest in Pieces

Murder at Monticello

Pay Dirt

Murder, She Meowed

Murder on the Prowl

Cat on the Scent

Sneaky Pie's Cookbook
for Mystery Lovers

Pawing Through the Past

Claws and Effect

Catch as Cat Can

The Tail of the Tip-Off

Whisker of Evil

Cat's Eyewitness

Sour Puss

Puss 'n Cahoots

The Purrfect Murder

Santa Clawed

Animal Magnetism

Mickey, a few years before I was born. *Photo by Julia Buckingham Brown.*

Animal
Magnetism

My Life with Creatures
Great and Small

Rita Mae Brown

BALLANTINE BOOKS TRADE PAPERBACKS
NEW YORK

A 2010 Ballantine Books Trade Paperback Edition

Copyright © 2009 by American Artists, Inc.

All rights reserved.

Published in the United States by Ballantine Books, an imprint of The Random House
Publishing Group, a division of Random House, Inc., New York.

BALLANTINE and colophon are registered trademarks of Random House, Inc.

Originally published in hardcover in the United States by Ballantine Books, an imprint
of The Random House Publishing Group, a division of Random House, Inc., in 2009.

ISBN 978-0-345-51180-5

Printed in the United States of America

www.ballantinebooks.com

1 2 3 4 5 6 7 8 9

Book design by Susan Turner

Dedicated to
those who have been saved by an animal
and who saved one in return.

Contents

Introduction

*P*urring, deep rumbling, is my first memory of life. Mickey, a long-haired tiger cat, provided the purr as he slept in my cradle. Mother called him an Angora. These days people call them Persians.

Looking back, I realize that my whole life has been lived with and through animals. Other people's significant dates include first kiss, first physical congress and attendant drama, first marriage, first child, first job—well, you get the idea. For me, it's first cat, first dog, first horse, first cow, and so on. And each of them taught me something.

This book is about the many lessons I've learned, the animals who have loved me, endured me, and taught me, and my bottomless love for them in return.

The past rides on my shoulder like the parrot my paternal grandmother kept. What a chatterbox that bird was. Never on good terms with the old biddy, one summer I taught her parrot to say unchristian words. The past is like that: whispering, chattering, squawking, and often the very things you'd prefer not to hear or remember.

As Mickey was first, let me start there with what he taught me. He could run, jump, hear, smell, and probably taste better than I could. I'd crawl on the floor to try and catch him. He'd let me reach his luxuriant tail, then hop away. Taunting me gave him great pleasure.

Mickey taught me how to play, and how to see the world through all of my senses.

Once I could walk without falling down, my life became an endless stream of adventures. Back then, I lacked a sharp sense of time passing and had no concept of deadlines. It was a delicious state that modern life quickly obliterates. Mickey's timeframe was my timeframe. My goal is to return to that early delight, that freedom from the clock, and to be more like cats. It's a formidable task.

Mickey and I took our constitutionals, Mother's term. Hers covered more ground: four miles in the morning and two or three at sunset. Mickey and I loitered under lilacs in bloom. He'd leap straight up to catch a black swallowtail, which usually got away. We'd climb maples and oaks. We'd jump into leaf piles in the fall, which meant that Dad had to rake them all up again. He never minded, and a few times he jumped in with us. Mickey played catch with my jack balls. We'd read together and we always slept together. I still need a cat for a good night's sleep.

My Aunt Mimi (Louise to those of you who have read the "Six of One" series) had many dogs throughout her life. She had a lovely Boston Bull, as large as a boxer, named Butch. Butch and Mickey coexisted, since one sister was usually in the company of the other. And the three of us were fast friends, showing that different species can indeed get along.

My aunt conceived of herself as the Virgin Mary but she had also conceived two daughters. Mother called her Divergent

Mary. Her dogs played as important a role in my life as my own pets did. Usually I trained her dogs, too. Never could train Aunt Mimi.

One day when I was eight, Mother took me by the hand. Mickey, now an elderly gentleman, was failing. She placed him in his little crate and we waited atop Queen Street Hill for the bus. Only rich people owned more than one car. Dad needed ours. The veterinarian's office squatted close to the Mason–Dixon Line. I remember walking into the tidy white clapboard building, a sense of foreboding filtering through me. I was determined not to cry.

Mother accompanied Mickey. I languished in the waiting room. When she came out, Mickey was wrapped in a lemon-yellow towel in his crate.

Once home, the sun still bright, we buried him under the large blooming crabapple tree up by the old pasture. The air carried all the messages of spring, Mickey's favorite season. Not until the last pat of the shovel did Mom give way. I let loose, too.

Mickey taught me my first great lesson in life, which is that one animal or person can touch many others. I'd thought only of my relationship with Mickey, not Mother's. Not once did it occur to me that she loved him before I came into the world. He was her shadow then.

To this day I don't like lemon-colored towels. I adore tiger cats and crabapple trees. A tiger cat is sitting with me now. If I can find the money this spring I am going to realize a dream and line one of my farm roads with crabapples. Mickey would approve.

Not all the animals I have learned from were mine. And some of the most profound lessons came from spending time with people who were blessed with the gift to understand and appreciate God's creatures.

My grandfather kept foxhounds given to him by his brother, Bob, who was a kennelman of the Green Spring Valley Hunt. PopPop Harmon returned from World War I a far different man than when he'd entered it. As long as Big Mimi was alive, she held him together. She died in 1948 and he went to pieces, drinking enough to float a battleship. Couldn't hold a job so he made a little money entering hunting contests.

When I visited, he put the liquor aside. Not until I was an adult did I fathom how he protected me from his affliction and what it must have cost him to do so. If I was especially good I could eat with the foxhounds and sleep with them, too. They were American foxhounds (along with some Crossbreds), which is what I now have in my kennels for the Oak Ridge Hunt Club. Through PopPop's hounds I learned the basics of canine communication, which is quite sophisticated.

For instance, a well-mannered person says "Excuse me" or "Pardon me" if someone blocks their path. A dog bumps another dog and, given the hierarchical nature of canines, the younger or lesser dog moves. Young and small, I had to gain the respect of the hounds. If a hound didn't move out of my way, I bumped him.

When a hound or house dog brought me a toy and I asked the animal to release it, if he didn't, I'd chastise him. Asking for the toy is a signal to play. Sometimes I pretended I wanted that slobbery toy and I would chase the dog. Then I'd stop, turn my back, and walk away. The dog would follow, toy in mouth. This would go on until one of us pooped out, and it always made the dog so happy.

Spontaneous play draws the participants closer together. This is one of the things humans lose as they get older. Given all the responsibilities people acquire in life, it's difficult to be spontaneous. Dogs, cats, and horses don't punch a time clock. They don't need to turn in reports or expense accounts. Every now and then it's good to walk away from whatever burdens you, pick up a ball, and throw it for the dog.

Tone of voice matters. If a dog speaks low to another dog—not a growl, just a low tone—all is usually well. If the pitch rises, it means excitement. The danger bark is distinctive and doesn't sound like either of the above. People often raise their voices when talking to their dogs or children. The dog gets fired up, jumps up or runs around, and the person then tells the dog to stop. But the person started it. It's not the dog's fault.

Each species has its own sophisticated communication system. Animals learn ours but we rarely learn theirs, and then we punish them for not understanding, or we call them stupid.

There's no such thing as a dumb dog, but God knows there are continents filled with dumb humans.

Sometimes I am one of those dumb humans, so I know whereof I speak. I learned how hounds work in a pack and saw that humans do, too. Hounds' expansive ability to love carried me through many a crisis, including PopPop's death. The hounds knew he was dying and I learned very early to trust their diagnosis. If you know what to look for, you, too, can see.

My hounds knew before I did when my best friend, Dr. Herbert Jones, the sustaining love of my life, was failing. When he died—my Gibraltar shattered, sinking into an ocean of grief—I went to my hounds and slept beside them, right in the kennel. It gave me strength to face the next day.

On my farm, if a hound passes its prime, he or she stays on. They've shown me that retirement isn't a good thing for hounds and is probably worse for people. So I find jobs for them.

All throughout my life, I've observed, tried to be flexible, tried to learn new languages. My first horse, not really mine but a draft horse, a big gray Percheron, taught me to think like a prey animal. Being a medium-sized predator, I found this difficult. Suzie Q, the horse, was better at understanding me than I was at understanding her.

Franklin, Mother Brown's parrot, possessed a wicked sense of humor. Bird intelligence can be frightening when they cock their heads and glare at you with those glittering eyes. The pterodactyl is never far behind. Franklin, who liked me, would set up a ruckus in his cage so Mamaw would let him out and we'd go around together. Mickey was not allowed to visit her. Just as well, or Franklin would have spoken his last line. What a chatterbox he was.

While trying to understand Franklin's mind I studied him when he was watching other birds. Those brains are small but filled with dense wiring. I still do not know how they communicate in flocks. Oh, sure, I know Canada geese honk, but there's more to it than that. Usually, I do know what they're saying in general: the call note which is a kind of "howdy do," the true song sometimes sung in duet but so seamlessly that people assume it is one bird, the "git out" curse and the true fear note which can cut through steel. It seems birds and other animals can predict the weather. Understanding the fear note and watching birds and other creatures take to high ground helped me to get my stock to high ground when a hurricane swept through after the weatherman predicted it would not go inland.

I owe talkative Franklin a lot. Thanks to Franklin, I have a strong suspicion that humans, freed from technology and again utilizing our senses, could communicate in flocks and without much fuss. We could also send messages across the oceans without ever picking up a phone or touching a computer.

Humans can do this. The natives of Australia can send messages to one another wherever they are in the world. But we can, too. Haven't you ever felt a strong compulsion to call someone? You do and the individual says, "I was just thinking about you." Or they are in distress and your call comes at a crucial time. Whether we can reclaim this faded ability and exercise it at will, I don't know. It may even be possible for different species to do this. You may be able to pick up something from your dog. I don't know, but it seems possible. Whenever there is deep emotion, there's a connection.

This book is about the sweep and sweepings of a life lived close to nature and lived with deep respect and sometimes fear of earth's other residents. I've looked a bobcat in the eye and recognized my better. I've come up on a bear and felt gratitude that he decided to run. I've paid my last respects to beloved hounds, horses, and cats with both sorrow and joy, and felt profoundly grateful that I could ease their passage into the beyond, something I couldn't do for my own mother.

Given that this involves my family and my human friends, there are sexual peccadilloes, gambling problems, drinking problems (not mine, I can be stupid all by myself, I don't need help), catnip addictions. There's thievery, which is practiced as much by the dogs as the cats, plus a few folks are doing it, too, and foxes: lots of foxes, most especially Sardine, who, as you might suspect, likes sardines. She likes my chickens, too.

There is a criminal chicken. Shocking, but you'll see we aren't the only creatures who can be hateful.

There's a Catholic fox who lives near an Episcopalian fox, with interactions that remind me of my own family, for I have heard heated exchanges of a less than charitable nature. If there aren't foxes in heaven I don't want to go. Of course, I may not be going anyway. I'm a bad Christian, but I'm too old to be a good anything else.

Bad Christian or not, much of what I am is a result of a life with and close to animals. I hope this book does them justice, for they have done right by me.

Animal Magnetism

Me at five, holding Skippy (there were a lot of Skippys!).
Photo by Julia Buckingham Brown.

Money Isn't Everything—Love Is

From the time I could put two thoughts together, I knew that I wanted a foxhound of my very own. My grandfather (Pop-Pop) and great-uncle Bob Harmon had kept American foxhounds for years and I was crazy about them. But my dad, granddad, and great-uncle thought that at six, I was too young to handle American foxhounds. They are tremendously sensitive and possess phenomenal drive. So they decided on a Chesapeake Bay Retriever for my first puppy, my first training experience. Turned out to be a wise choice, for they are easy dogs.

Chaps, along with PopPop's hounds, taught me how to communicate with dogs. More importantly, he taught me about love. He also had a great sense of humor. He'd steal my baseball glove, he'd bring me what were to him treats (a deer leg), plus if a puddle of water presented itself, he'd dive in. He always wanted me in the puddle, creek, or river with him.

I learned not to doubt Chaps. His senses, keener than mine, proved an early warning system. He'd lift his head, open his nostril, and gather information. Or, like the foxhounds, he'd put his nose to ground.

Not until I was in my late teens did I realize I understood

dog communication, thanks to Chaps, and thanks to PopPop and G-uncle (G for Great) Bob. Canines, cats, and horses have many more ways to communicate than we do. Ears swivel, pupils dilate or contract, hackles rise or fall, tails wag or stand straight out, and the range of sounds they absorb and react to is wide. Their acute hearing picks up a tiny gurgle from a mouse as well as the snort of a stag a quarter of a mile away. Fortunately for me, hearing is my strongest sense, nudging into the cat and canine range but still well beneath their powers. When I was five I heard things. Mother thought I was expressing imagination. Finally, she took me to a doctor for tests. She realized then that I wasn't making things up.

Chaps, born into the long-standing contract between humans and dogs, played his part. I learned to play mine. He'd run ahead, stop, look at me, and say, "It's safe up to this point." Most people don't realize what their dogs are telling them when they run ahead and stop. Now, this isn't true with a pack of foxhounds, although it can be true with a foxhound kept as a pet. Their job is to put those noses down and pick up scent. But pets, the dogs that live with people, continually warn, protect, look out for their owners. So often the owners don't get it.

The human part of the contract is this: you share food, nurse them when they're sick, give them a warm, clean place to sleep, and a quiet passage out of life when they become too feeble or face pain.

As I was learning all of this I was loving every minute of it. I found I could communicate with animals better than with people. Actually, I didn't communicate with people, at least not grown-ups, for I am of that generation that was sternly instructed, "Don't speak unless spoken to." Most of my childhood was spent silently observing, good practice for a writer. Good manners taught me silence and the animals taught me to observe without judgment. If an adult noticed me and began a conversation—usually with "How's school?" or "How's Chaps?"—then I could reply. However, I was not to ask questions. That would be rude. I could question the family (within reason) but no one outside of the family.

Chaps could smell emotional states. We give off scent but our olfactory organ is poor, so we can detect stinky sweat, the sweat of fear, or the opposite, cleanliness, or fragrant flowers, but not much more. Consider that a foxhound has about one hundred million scent receptors. You and I bump along with ten million. We can't imagine the texture, the medley of odors that an ordinary canine can process, understand, act upon. They even have the ability to process how long ago scent was laid. It's a dazzling gift the gods have given them.

They have another great gift: the ability to love. Chaps loved me, even when I was distant and just walking down a dirt road, oblivious to his overtures. He loved me when I was mean, which wasn't often. He didn't require that I be beautiful (good thing), smart, witty, or a fascinating conversationalist. He loved me and I loved him.

I taught Chaps to retrieve using duck wings. PopPop brought me a duck wing that one of his duck hunting buddies gave him, since he knew I wanted one. He tied it to a fishing line and gave me his old fly rod. I'd cast the wing, then reel it in. Soon, for he was a smart fellow, Chaps would run after the wing if I cast it. I had to put a little sinker on it because the wing was so light it just fluttered. With the sinker I could send it out there. When Chaps dropped the wing at my feet or let me take it from his mouth, I'd give him a little treat. Mother cooked up meat treats, then dried them. Now these things are available commercially.

This is not to say I can train gun dogs, but I could probably learn. Chaps showed me the basics. Dad said I could sell him for seventy-five dollars, which was a lot of money. PopPop Harmon praised me. I'm not sure I did all that much, since retrieving was bred into Chaps, but I lapped up the praise. I didn't want the money. I cried. I begged Dad to let me keep Chaps. He did. Mother said I'd never learn the value of a penny if I didn't earn some—this coming from a woman whose money burned a hole in her pocket. But she loved Chaps, too, so Mickey, Chaps, and later Tuffy, another tiger cat, and I lived together until Chaps, at the age of five, developed a liver condition.

He was so young. I knew enough to understand it would be cruel to keep him going when he'd only go downhill. Once again we visited the vet by the Mason-Dixon Line, only this time Dad drove us. I accompanied my friend. He kissed me. Surely he knew this was an act of grace. I cried. I couldn't help it, and God bless him, the vet cried, too. Chaps left earth peacefully and without pain. The force of grief as well as gratitude was beginning to be part of my emotional development.

I know I do not have as big a heart as Chaps or most any dog. Humans don't. We are cursed with ego, selfishness, and ignorance, overlaid with arrogance. We try. At least some of us do. If I could love to the level of Chaps, I reckon I'd be a saint.

Chaps, while he taught me how to communicate with dogs, taught me most about love. I can't live without the love of dogs. I don't know how anyone can.

Aunt Mimi's Butch. *Photo by Julia Buckingham Brown.*

Animals Can Save Your Life

T hanks to a scrappy fox terrier named King Edward, I learned at the age of six that animals can save your life. They can also help you to stick up for yourself.

King Edward, Ed for short, was owned by Mother's good friend Diddy Pocahontas (I will refrain from using her real last name should some distant relative be one step ahead of a running fit). Diddy swore she owed her life to King Edward because before she found the lump he'd kept poking at her bosom. Once she realized something wasn't right, she marched into the doctor's, thereby losing her bosom but keeping her life. She never doubted King Edward after that.

Diddy did not get her missing bosom rebuilt. This was in the early fifties and plastic surgery was in its infant stages. She used the empty cup of her bra for a purse. In the warm months she'd wear low-cut bodices, reach in and fish out her money. No one said anything except her mother, Mary, who continually urged her to wear a falsie.

Diddy's response was, "You can always tell how much money I have by looking at my bosom."

Mary's response goes unrecorded. It wasn't charitable.

Mary, getting grand in her sixties, told anyone who would listen that she was a descendant of the original Pocahontas, whose bones lay safely in the Episcopal churchyard which she visited frequently. She visited it frequently because only the dead would have her. She was a holy terror who couldn't help bullying her own daughter and anyone else who got in her way. King Edward couldn't stand her. And if your four-footed friend doesn't like someone, pay attention. They aren't worth liking.

Now, Mother was the hub of social and political activity in two counties, Carroll County, Maryland, and York County, Pennsylvania. One of her sayings was "Keep your friends close, your enemies closer." She shepherded many friends and not a few enemies. Everyone had dogs, cats, horses, birds, and most of the local farmers ran cattle. Mother prided herself on knowing everyone, and that included pets and work animals. One June, she organized a picnic. People outnumbered June bugs. She had guests that were newborn and two in their nineties. Julia Brown threw a great party. She was never short on guests.

Everyone brought their dogs. Butch, my aunt's Boston Terrier, was there, and Tiny, Lila Meeney's dachshund, along with Diddy's King Edward and Chaps, my Chesapeake Bay Retriever. He was four then. So many dogs. I loved it. As the decibel level increased, the dogs retreated, for the noise troubled them.

What was causing such a ruckus? Turns out someone from Other Parts (not Virginia, not Maryland) stupidly tried to press Mary for the truth about her connection to the original Pocahontas.

We all knew that the original Pocahontas, called "Poke" by Mother, had died in London and was probably buried there. But we knew better than to say this in front of Mary. Back then Southern women could faint at the drop of a hat. Some ladies were prone to a genteel swoon where the lady in question would sway, drop to her knees, and flop over, thereby escaping injury. Others went down like a ship hit below the water line, accompanied by moans, groans, or silent suffering. That's why people such as Mother—remember, she pretty much ran both sides of the Mason-Dixon Line—carried smelling salts. She'd kneel and press the hanky with the smelling salts under the lady's nose. Eyelids would flutter. The spectators would fan the lady. If she was well built, the men fanned vigorously. Southerners, even now, understand that life is theater. A good faint might be considered a social skill.

So during our June picnic, when Mary was challenged on her illustrious tribal heritage, she sank like a stone. She lay there awhile before Mother realized few people wished her to revive. She dutifully cracked the smelling salts into her hanky and kneeled down, just as King Edward lifted his leg. Mary shot up, shouting, "Diddy, I will kill that worthless dog. I will strangle him. I will strangle you." It went on. Diddy rolled her eyes—"Oh, la"—which further inflamed her mother.

Whether or not Diddy consumed Dutch courage I don't know. I could tell if someone was three sheets to the wind but I couldn't determine if they'd only knocked back a drink or two. Perhaps Diddy did just that and King Edward's comment on her supine mother emboldened her.

I'd never heard a proper lady cuss in public before. Diddy scorched the earth. "I am sick and tired of eating your shit." That was for starters. Mary, eyes big as eight balls, screamed back, "I brought you into this world, I can take you out."

We could have sold tickets to that show, which wound up with a totally revived Mary chasing Diddy down to the pond. Diddy escaped in a canoe, King Edward jumped in, her mother stood on the shore cursing Diddy, King Edward, and the entire assembled crowd. Sure was a good picnic.

Later, Mary consoled herself with sherry laced with something stronger. You see, a lady couldn't luxuriate in a straight shot of bourbon or scotch, as it would excite comment. So Mary, her slender flask tucked into her stocking, discreetly poured the contents into a glass of sherry. Of course we all knew but pretended that it wasn't happening. Skirts, long and flowing then, could hide plenty of objects, even people. The incongruity of a lady hiding her drinking but swearing like a fishmonger was also overlooked.

Soon Mary was out cold, lying on a blanket. No bucket was necessary. She had a hollow leg. She'd not throw up, for which I was grateful.

Diddy rowed back in, chin up, face radiant. She and her friend Lila Meeney, both good-looking women with good racks (although Diddy sported half a rack), danced, laughed, and frolicked. Lila belonged to the Man-of-the-Month Club and her pick for June was Carter Farley, a fellow of average intelligence and above-average looks.

Diddy sat down with King Edward on her lap. The summer dress, thin cotton, cut low, allowed King Edward to delicately reach in and pull out bills with his teeth. No one thought a thing of it except Mary, and she was again dead to the world.

Mother moved through the crowd gathering support for a zoning variance. A small company wanted to build something really new called air conditioners and Mother thought it was a good idea.

The picnic roared on, twilight adding even more allure to the gathering. Despite Diddy's missing boob, men found her attractive. Freed of her mother's constant judgment, ready for anything after her public fuss with Mary, she openly flirted with Rupert, Rupe for short. He was the Esso station owner, a nice man, even if he did always have grease under his fingernails. I was already fond of Rupe because he was one of the few adults who actually invited me to ask questions once I told him how much I liked motors. He owned a boxer, Spike. Spike and King Edward were great friends and it was apparent that Rupe and Diddy were becoming great friends, too.

Mother said you could tell because the dogs got along so well. Obviously, they'd been keeping company on the sly.

Meanwhile, Lila and Carter, Tiny trailing along, had wandered off in the starlight.

Mary began to revive as the temperature cooled down. She opened her eyes to see Rupe put his arm around Diddy's waist. She blinked, sat up, none the worse for wear. She harangued Diddy that she could do better than a grease monkey.

Diddy didn't bother to fight but simply said, "Mother, shut up. I'm doing what I want."

King Edward growled and Spike looked on in amazement. Diddy turned on her heel, Rupe and the two dogs following in her wake. Mary stood up only to crumple down. Too much bourbon—I mean sherry.

Lila, Carter in tow, walked back to the group upon hearing the ruckus. Mary turned on her. "Slut" fell out of Mary's mouth. Worse fell out of Lila's. Tiny emerged from underneath Lila's skirt to attack Mary. He bit her ankles. Mary screamed she'd get rabies.

That was how Mary came to have the rabies shots in her stomach even though Tiny was a perfectly healthy dachshund.

Mary wanted attention. She reported a vicious dog to the sheriff, who wrote it all down. Then when Mary left his office he tossed it in the waste can.

Diddy married Rupe. Mary pulled herself together to be the mother of the bride. It was an October wedding. Both dogs attended the reception, also going along on the honeymoon.

What a lovely man Rupe was, and he made Diddy happy, even as Mary fussed that Diddy married beneath her. Rupe overlooked his mother-in-law and I came to understand that people like Mary, funny though they may be, are utterly miserable inside. Anyone who can't embrace life is a sorry soul and they'll make you sorry, too.

When King Edward died in 1954, Diddy cried. Rupe did, too, but the person who went all to pieces was Mary Pocahontas. Funny.

King Edward saved Diddy's life, not only by finding the lump in her breast, but also by showing her that it was possible to stand up to her mother. If Ed hadn't helped her find her backbone, she would've missed out on a rich life with Rupe. And we would have missed out on that unforgettable picnic.

Rudy and Godzilla curled up together. *Photo by Judy Pastore.*

Courtship and Mating

Mother had a refreshingly low opinion of monogamy. Naturally, one did one's best. If a wild moment came upon you, the best course of action was to be discreet, she would explain to her sister, Mimi.

Aunt Mimi would glow with indignation. Of course, Mother knew that Sister, as she called her, gave herself up to the thrill of infidelity once in the 1930s. Naturally, my aunt suffered amnesia on this issue.

Mother pointed out that many animals, like the human, are not monogamous, while others are. She also pointed out that marriage provides camouflage. Produce an heir and a spare and then do what you will. Just be careful. None of which means you don't honor and love your husband. Hopefully, you do. However, Mother couldn't fathom how anyone whose blood temperature hung at 98.6°F wouldn't occasionally be attracted by another man. Then again, Mother was a bold spirit who knew that all ideologies, whether religious or governmental, exist to take you away from yourself. Her advice was always "Keep your mouth shut and do what you want." She certainly did.

Mother was a keen observer of nature, and thanks to her example, I was fascinated by the behavior of animals. Clearly cats, dogs, and horses didn't mate for life. But geese seemed to be quite faithful, and I noticed that the foxes stuck together until the cubs left, which in Maryland and Virginia is usually late October. Then the male might leave the den or he might not.

Watching foxes as a child, I also learned that the breeding cycle was tied to the food supply. I couldn't figure out how they knew what the food supply would be when the cubs were born and growing. Here in central Virginia, foxes typically breed in early January. Usually those are the grays; they start before the reds. The reds come courting late January and February. How do they know? We sure don't. We can develop the most sophisticated weather instruments and we make many predictions: we are inaccurate. But the fox knows.

I'd talk about these things with Mother. She never said I was foolish or that I pestered her with stupid questions. She loved nature. My curiosity and study delighted her. A good thing, too, because I wasn't turning into the kind of daughter she had envisioned, which is to say a smaller model of herself: a femme fatale. However, we shared enough that we could spend time happily together. Her view of foxes was we would never understand them because we (meaning science at that time) considered them vermin. Vermin don't rate study or government grants. Everything I know about foxes I have learned from Mother, PopPop, or my own observation.

The monogamy issue puzzled me. I noticed over the years that some dog foxes (that is, the males) would leave the den when the cubs did. But they would return to the female for breeding season. There was a bond between some of them. The boys would leave, but the half-grown girls often stayed close, building dens near the parent couple. I'd eagerly give Mother the news about this. I built little scent stations to count the paw prints. Often you can distinguish between paws and thereby get an idea of how many foxes crossed your station. All it takes is a two-foot square of sand or dirt smoothed out. You pour fox urine on it. Most hunting/outdoor stores carry small bottles of it. Deer hunters use it to mask human scent from deer. What an unwise move if the foxhounds are running. I saw this nearly ruin a hunt once. The poor foxhounds thought, "My, what a queer fox." The human thought, "Oh, shit."

Every day, come back to the scent station, count the prints, smooth it out, refresh the odor. I'd do this at the end of October when the cubs, especially the males, usually disperse. Latitude determines dispersement. If you are in Genesee Valley Hunt territory outside of Rochester, New York, probably you'd do this earlier. If you're hunt staff for Misty Morning Hounds in Gainesville, Florida, you'd probably make the station much later.

When mating season came, I'd bundle up and watch. Some males, mostly young ones, couldn't find a female or were chased off by a bigger male. Foxes, like dogs, have identifiable features. You can often tell them apart. The next year, that former young fellow would be bigger, and sure enough, he'd find a girlfriend. I asked Mother if they loved each other. She thought about this and declared she expected they loved each other better than some human pairs, probably not as much as others.

Foxes, like cats, are not herd or pack animals. But they have a family feeling. I liked watching the family grow.

As I was coming to grips with mating, I started looking at humans. Men lowered their voices, women raised theirs. Men pushed their shoulders back. A woman often dropped a shoulder slightly in the presence of a male she found attractive so as to make him seem taller. This fascinated me as much as watching foxes.

Once you know what to look for, who is attracted to whom is glaringly obvious. And, as in all the higher vertebrates, the woman controls the deal.

Poor men. So many of them can't read the signs, continually running into walls and becoming, I'm sure, frustrated and sad. Women don't like high-pitched voices in men. Nor do they like men who cut them off physically. By this I mean (this usually happens in the teenage years, as the boys get smarter over time, most of them), a young man will put his arm against a wall thereby preventing a woman moving past it. Girls flat-out hate it. The other thing girls hate is when a young man thrusts his pelvis forward. I'm not sure this is a conscious action. It's obvious what it means and it's mating behavior. But women, often being better socialized than men (under more physical scrutiny), are appalled. It's just too damned obvious. I'd run back to Mother with my latest observation to be greeted with peals of laughter. I also noticed that boys become loud to attract female attention. It sure does attract attention, but not always in a positive manner.

The foxes were more subtle than the humans. The horses weren't. An older or tougher horse would chase a young one away if people were foolish enough to leave an intact male or males in with females. The female can and will break a stallion's leg if she's so inclined. Once again the male pays, and this time with his life.

Sometimes a stallion will bite a female on the neck and savage her, but if she can lash out she will. They should never be left together. Equine breeding should be monitored and controlled as a kindness. Fox courtship and mating seemed more affectionate than the equine variety.

With the passage of decades, I have come to the conclusion that many men can't read women at all, whereas women can almost always read men. And while my mother may have been a heretic to monogamy, she'd grumble if a married man was stupid enough to tip his hand. She could always tell, and now I could, too.

She'd point out to me what our neighbor Earl was doing and why his wife was blind as a bat. I'd reply maybe she didn't want to know. Mother gave me points for that insight. Life is easier if you deny painful things, at least for a time. Small wonder that drink, drugs, and various obsessions gain such control over us.

I noticed, especially among the horses, that mares would become devoted to one another, geldings, too. Mother's response to this was, "Love who you will but marry and produce children." She understood the human animal. Love is the wild card of existence.

As I pondered monogamy I ran smack into racism via separate fountains, motels, bus seats. As to most children of any race, it was confusing and very unsettling. At least I had the advantage of being Caucasian, so I wasn't thrown to the back of the bus, but I became upset that others were. I said to Mother that it was stupid and she agreed but she also said she didn't know how to change it. Then she said something that once again brought me back to animals: "Honey, it doesn't matter if a cat is black or white so long as it catches mice."

Many years later, her Chesterfield stapled to her lips, red with her favorite lipstick, I mentioned to her what I learned from foxes and her.

I said, "I've come to the conclusion that monogamy is contrary to nature but necessary for the greater social good."

She took a deep drag, her big poodle at her feet, laughed, and replied, "Aren't you the smartypants?"

Peaches, the house clown.

Every Animal Has a Gift

Mother told me every animal has a gift, and that gift keeps it alive. I could easily see a cat's gifts. There are so many: a cat can turn on a dime and give you a nickel's change. Their eyesight is much better than ours as are their hearing and sense of smell. Add to this the fact that cats don't give a damn. They'll do as they please.

The sheer athletic ability of a feline is astonishing. Foxes display much the same agility, although they can't jump quite as high as cats. At least, I've never seen one do so. But I've seen them jump straight up and twist over backwards to land on their feet. Impressive.

Foxes fascinated me as a child. Still do. If I didn't have my retriever Chaps with me on a walk, they'd pop out of their dens to look at me. A bark or little gurgle might let me know their opinion of me. Sometimes a fox would walk along with me about twenty yards off. As they are omnivorous, whatever I chewed on interested them. I'd leave out hard candy or pieces of my sandwich. This found favor with them. In many ways, a fox is like a dog: intelligent, curious. But they hunt differently than dogs do, which I figured out by following the gun dogs, usually English

Setters or small Irish Setters. Some of these setters were red and white, and are now recognized as a separate breed by the AKC.

Foxes hunt like cats. They stay still, then pounce. If there's snow on the ground they'll cock their ear in one direction, then the other, only to pounce in the middle where imaginary sound lines intersect, for they can hear the mice under the snow. This only works if the snow is light on the ground so there's air and tunnels. If it slicks down like vanilla icing, the mice stay in their nests. Who wouldn't?

I also realized that the fox mind works more quickly than my own. Yes, humans gave us the Brandenburg Concertos, *As You Like It,* the Sistine Chapel, etc., yet grand as these contributions are, you can't eat them. Even if a fox could write the vulpine *War and Peace* I doubt he or she would. What's the point? We need distractions and lessons in a way no other species seems to, which, as a child, I found confusing. I loved to read, I'd even read to the foxes and the birds. Mickey and Chaps would sit and listen and sometimes the wild animals would tilt their heads and listen for a time. I expect my cadence held their attention.

What mystified me was this: What is the human gift? I'm still working on that. What I was told in school proved untrue. My teachers would trumpet the superiority of the human animal. Point one: we walk upright. That's a recipe for slowness and a bad back later in life. Point two: we create tools and other species don't. Apparently, my teachers never watched a blackbird, a monkey, or even a house cat use an object to acquire what they want. Then came the big revelation of the opposable thumb. It's helpful, but it isn't the end-all be-all. Finally, they seized upon language.

Chaps understood nouns and verbs. How many, I didn't know, but he knew language, even though he couldn't reproduce it. The draft horses and mules in my life clearly understood commands in English. Humans do seem to have a more sophisticated level of language skills, but I suspect that this is as much a curse as a gift.

Mostly it's noise. Few people say anything of consequence and mostly they talk about themselves or their family. Nothing too original there, but being another human, one must listen and pretend the news is incredibly fresh. For any of us, probably one percent of our talking life we've uttered something profound or important. I count myself in that number. My advantage is I don't talk much unless I am called upon to give a speech.

Mother, shoving me into cotillion, harangued me to be a good conversationalist. I can do it. Hell, after twelve years of various forms of cotillion plus her relentless instruction, I'd be a blistering idiot if I couldn't chat. That doesn't mean I like it one bit more than when I was a child.

When I would sit a ways from the fox dens, I could hear them chattering inside. Sometimes one would come out and chatter at me. It wasn't a "Get out of here, Two Legs" bark. It was "Hi" or "You won't believe what my wife just did." By age seven I knew the difference. Yet the fox, for all its intelligence, evidenced no need to say much more.

The one time a fox isn't intelligent is if you give the distress call. There are little wooden horns, sort of like geese call horns, that make the fox distress noise. They'll run out to help, and in this way they are trapped. I am bitterly opposed to trapping unless it's a humane trap. John Morris, who works with me, traps our foxes so we can get the rabies and distemper shots in them. We can only trap them once in the Havahart traps. They know the drill after that. Since chasing foxes is the grand passion of my life, their well-being matters. I'm proud of Oak Ridge Fox Hunt

Club's work in keeping them healthy. Hunt staff perform numerous services that benefit pet owners, but we don't advertise our efforts. People in our territories, much less cities, don't realize that in a small way we are reducing the incidence of rabies, distemper, and mange in these beautiful creatures. (And no, we don't kill foxes in our foxhunts, so don't get your knickers in a knot.)

Bird plumage never goes out of fashion. *Photo by Judy Pastore.*

The Purpose of Plumage

Aunt Mimi's best friend, apart from Mother and Delphine Falkenroth, was Butch, her Boston Terrier, which she insisted on calling a Boston Bull. A large fellow, Butch was always the picture of elegance in his "tuxedo." But appearances can be deceiving, because he did not always behave like a gentleman. The two of them went everywhere together, except for the garden club because once Butch ate some tulip bulbs belonging to Mrs. Mundis. Aunt Mimi muttered they weren't worth squat, but nonetheless to keep the peace she paid Mrs. Mundis, who was well off, and she no longer brought Butch to garden club. Just as well, because the lectures bored him, which is why he ate the tulip bulbs in the first place.

I have written elsewhere, in fictional form, of the fierce competition at the garden shows. Aunt Mimi, famed for her daffodils as well as her beautiful clothing, spiked her daffs with gin. What bright happy daffodils they were. My aunt, a very attractive woman, declared alcohol never touched her lips. We always knew when she had "tested" her daffodil mixture because Butch would refuse to kiss her.

Both Mother and Aunt Mimi suffered from lead foot. Put them behind the wheel of any machine—tractor, car, motorcycle—and you burnt the wind. If Mother wasn't riding shotgun, Butch was. He loved to go "bye byes," and the only time Aunt Mimi evidenced any inclination to keep to sensible speeds around corners was when Butch was her passenger, because he'd fall over. I had to sit in the back. The dog came first.

My esteemed aunt's driving capabilities were so well known in the county that when people spied her coming down the road in the opposite direction they pulled over. Pedestrians moved far off the road. She'd wave, nod, and smile but she rarely slowed down.

One frosty moonlit night, Aunt Mimi was driving Mother, Butch, and me back from some ameliorative function. Those two took part in so many committees, fundraisers, social events, I couldn't keep track, and this one ran way late. As we reached the town square a young woman, swaddled in a heavy coat and scarf, wearing fashionable high-heeled shoes despite the cold, slowly trawled the sidewalk.

Aunt Mimi sniffed, "Only owls and whores are abroad this time of night."

"What's a whore?"

Mother quickly replied, "A whore is a woman who sells her body to men."

"Julia, don't tell her that!"

Mother considered this admonition. "Don't worry about it, kid. Big cities have whores. In the country we do it for free."

"Juts!" Aunt Mimi peeled around the other side of the square a bit too fast, but we stayed upright.

I hugged Butch. He was accustomed to his human's behavior.

"Oh, Sis, she has to learn about these things sometime."

"Why would anyone pay?" My curiosity was getting the better of me.

"This isn't a proper topic for a child of your tender years." My aunt hit the know-it-all tone. "Suffice it to say that ladies of quality guard their virtue."

"Yes, ma'am." I noticed a lady in a ratty fur coat urinating against the side of a building. "Look, that lady is peeing standing up."

The square after nine at night had a certain amount of demi-monde traffic, which is putting it nicely.

"Don't look!" Aunt Mimi cried, too late.

"How can she do that?" I was completely fascinated, wondering if there was a trick I'd missed in learning to relieve myself.

"She is a he." Mother started to laugh.

"Juts, will you shut up?" Aunt Mimi started to laugh, too.

"If that person hadn't been going to the bathroom how would you know?"

Mother let out peals of laughter. "The coat, honey, the coat. No real woman would be caught dead in that tatty thing."

"And the makeup." Aunt Mimi now warmed to the subject. "Ladies of quality don't paint their faces, and when men do it, they always overdo. Always overdo the accessories, too."

"Now, Sis, we use lipstick and a hint of rouge."

"Lipstick." She refused to admit to rouge.

"When in trouble, buy new lipstick." Mother turned to face me in the backseat. "Remember that, kid. Might save you some day."

"Why would that man dress like a woman?" I wasn't giving up.

"Envy." Mother giggled.

A silence from the driver was finally broken. "You know, Juts, you've got a point there. Why else?"

"We get to wear silks and furs and pretty colors. What do they get? Blue, brown, gray, black. I'd perish from visual boredom. And let's not forget hats, gloves, purses, shoes in all different colors. What do they get? One wallet. It's better to be a woman."

They started a review of their women friends' clothing, color palettes, and house décor. I listened for a time but my mind flitted back to owls and other birds.

Some species change coat with the seasons, but no other animals flash about like birds. Who can forget the sight of a male cardinal in the snow? An iridescent indigo bunting darting out in front of you? Apart from the brightly colored birds there are the ones who blend in, like woodcocks. Even a turkey, fantail folded, can take a moment to discern because of the coloring. When the male unfolds his tail, it's impressive, for they are big birds with incredible eyesight. Even if you're in camouflage, still as a mouse, move your eyes and a turkey will see the whites and fly off. Anyone who can bag a turkey has my utmost respect.

Bird plumage never goes out of fashion. Mother's and Aunt Mimi's laughter about the transvestite's tatty coat told me I'd better make the right choices about my plumage. Mother didn't expect me to wear a tiara while driving the tractor, but she pounded into me the importance of dressing for the occasion. I used to do it but it's gotten too expensive. And one time about twenty years ago, a media escort said to me at a signing, "Do you want to look richer than your readers?"

Actually, I'd like to look a little dressed up, but the ordeals of air travel have made it all but impossible.

Bird displays send signals and so do our clothes. Even in this informal and sloppy age, clothes still make the man, and the woman. Aunt Mimi's dog always wore his tuxedo. Someday I think I'll show up at a formal event with a Boston Terrier and I'll wear a tuxedo, too. You'll recognize me because I'll be the one in heels.

Mother gave me her love of horses and nature. In the foreground is an old retiree, in the background is Gunsmoke, a Thoroughbred.
Photo by Danielle A. Durkin.

Mother's Gift of Nature

So many different kinds of owls lived near us or in the old outbuildings. We had barn owls, screech owls, the Great Horned Owl, and one hard winter we even had a white owl, the most beautiful bird I'd ever seen. I've never seen another one in these parts. That was in 1953.

If I was quiet in the winter, I was allowed to stay up and read late. In the summers, Mother allowed me to stay outside late. I'd listen to the owls talk. If they were angry or giving warning, the noise was harsh, hard on human ears. They'd coo and cackle happily, too. The mating calls were pretty, especially those of the Great Horned. I loved to listen to them answer one another.

People who aren't close to animals explain their behavior in utilitarian terms. I believe most of the higher vertebrates are capable of joy. Sometimes, hearing the owls, I felt they burbled, gurgled, and sang for the joy of being alive. This is especially obvious with songbirds such as cardinals.

When I was in school we were taught that the females are capable of singing, but only the males do it. This isn't true. Sometimes, if you listen carefully, the male may start a song, but then the female comes in and they sing a duet so finely tuned it sounds like one bird. The song is clear with distant cadence, long notes, short notes in predicable progression. It's an easy song for a human to whistle.

Their eyesight is so superior to ours, we can't imagine it, just like we can't imagine how fast a fox processes information. Birds fly high, diving down to grab a mouse or a fish. Not the seed eaters but the flesh eaters. They fold their wings next to their bodies and dive. The waterbirds go straight into the water. The ground birds open their wings at the last moment and grab their prey feet first.

Owls have soft feathers. They fly silently. No rustle. A blackbird has noisy feathers. You can hear them overhead.

One crisp night in early winter I asked my mother, "How many owls do you know?"

"Ha. More than you. Put your coat on."

We bundled up. It was way past my bedtime but Mother could be flexible. I had to keep Mickey and Chaps inside. She said they'd spoil it.

We walked outside. The ground was hard with heavy frost. A stone bench was planted under a huge old hickory. We sat down. Soon enough we heard the owls calling to one another. Mother, a keen birder, identified the various notes. Some were "You're in my territory" calls. Others were a simple "Hi." A few registered complaints, loud and clear. Due to the cold, there were no insects. The only sounds were owls calling, the occasional bleat of a cow, and the rustling of a nocturnal creature. There weren't as many deer back then so I heard none. The deer are easy to identify by sound.

I often recall that bright, cold night when Mother eagerly shared her love of nature. She taught me to recognize many birdcalls. I might know fifty, sixty at most. I still have trouble sorting out the different warbler calls, but most birdcalls are very clear once you memorize them. A goldfinch or indigo bunting sounds nothing like a bluejay. There are some variations, though, in, say, a thrush. They express some individuality.

Bluejays can mimic, just like catbirds and mockingbirds. What fun to hear them. The bluejays in particular can be creative. They'll swoop near a bird feeder and sound like a ferocious predator bird. This scatters the little birds. Then down they pop to eat up everything. One spring day, Mother, on that same bench, whistled various tunes to a mockingbird, who reproduced them exactly.

Why? Does it matter? I am weary of people needing reasons. What mattered was that the mockingbird delighted Mother, myself, and apparently itself.

"Birds tell you the weather," Mother told me. "You know the birds that leave for winter. If they leave early, it will be an early winter. But all birds can tell you when storms are coming. They hop around and talk a lot way before the storm hits. Eat what they can. Then all of a sudden they're in their nests and cubbyholes. When it's quiet like that, won't be long."

As the decades have rolled on, I've continued to study birds. I'm hardly an expert. For one thing, my study often focuses on hunting. When I hunt my foxhounds, the birds are invaluable to me. If the goldfinches fill the bushes, along with other small birds, I know my fox has not passed by in the last fifteen minutes. If they're up in the trees and chattering, then they've been disturbed. Now, it may not be the fox that disturbed them, but something has, and I'd best be alert.

Blackbirds hate foxes. They'll mob them sometimes. They make a specific sound much like a mob of humans, whose reason, or at least sense of responsibility, seems to diminish the bigger the group gets. Shakespeare wrote scathingly of the mob, and he was right. Blackbirds seem to possess these same qualities. Their mobbing is hostile. If I hear that sound, I can be pretty sure my fox is moving and they are flying over him or her. But blackbirds also gossip. How they gossip. If only I knew what they were saying. You can hear them making a clicking sound, a happy sound as they merrily blather on. Then there's the distinctive call note. Most birds have a call note as well as a true song. I wouldn't say that blackbirds sing, but they do emit a series of notes that probably pass as a song among them. This music is precious to someone studying foxes.

Owls can tell you a lot about foxes, too. Sometimes they will shadow a fox, going from tree to tree or flying over the animal. Took me years to figure out why. It should have been obvious, but I never said I was smart. Foxes and owls hunt the same game. One can assist the other, whether it's intentional or not. An owl isn't going to swoop down and steal the fox's kill because the fox can and will catch it. Given the talons and a good-sized owl, this can be a bloody, costly struggle. But once the fox picks up its rabbit or mouse and moves on, the owl can fly down and kill any mice lurking about.

Occasionally I'll see raptors watching foxes, too, pretty much for the same reason as the owls. The raptors—hawks, falcons, and kites—have an Achilles' heel. Sooner or later, they have to let you know how important they are. And the sounds they make are truly distinctive, piercing and easy to read. The owls—maybe they are wiser—shut up. So do the foxes, for the most part.

We humans, like the raptors, belong to the babbling class. We even pay people to talk. This would astonish even the most garrulous blackbird. It astonishes me, but I like the paycheck.

Here I am on Peggy Sue, a beautiful Percheron who reminds me of my very first horse, Suzie Q.

My First Horse, Suzie Q

Many humans learn to feel love from a dog or cat. Not too many have felt it from a horse. The emotion is as big as the animal. Given my mother's great passion for horse racing and the fact that I lived in horse country, I had grown up around horses. But we didn't own any.

How desperately I wanted to ride.

"You'll ride after you learn to take care of horses," said Mother. "You'll muck stalls, feed, water, groom, pick up their hooves and clean them out. None of this just hopping on, young lady. There's a world of difference between being a horseman and being a rider. Riders are a dime a dozen. Horsemen are rare."

As a first-grader, no hack barn wanted me. They figured small, young, and dumb, and pretty much they were correct. Mother dutifully made the rounds seeing if she could find me a little work. A hack barn is a barn that rents horses by the day. There used to be loads of them. These days, thanks to our litigious age, few remain.

"Mother, maybe Mr. Byrd would let me work on the farm after school or before school."

Tweetie Byrd was a local farmer who owned over a thousand

acres of good soil, and lived quite comfortably. He ran to fat even though he worked hard. He was descended from the august Byrd family of Virginia. This fact crept into most conversations with Tweetie—that and the price of a bushel of corn.

Tweetie's Percheron draft, Suzie Q, had a beautiful dappled coat that was truly eye-catching. She was well made, well proportioned. And she looked at you with the kindest sweet brown eyes. I loved her.

"Tweetie, pay help?" she roared.

"If he let me ride Suzie Q, that would be my pay."

We were at the big open stall market during this discussion. A late-season cantaloupe filled her hand. She examined it and dropped it in her grocery bag. "You might have something there, kid."

Once home we put away the groceries. The Norge refrigerator made a racket in the kitchen. The springhouse could still keep milk and cheese cool, but the refrigerator was handier. Still, I didn't like it.

I swept out the kitchen, trying to be more than usually helpful. Since I had to be browbeaten into housework but would willingly perform outdoor chores, this seemed a big deal to me.

Mother laughed. "All right."

She skipped (yes, she skipped a lot) to the black phone in the hall. It was a party line. Our number was four digits. Mother complained it was hard to remember everyone's number because they used to be three digits. That was before I was born. Four seemed okay with me. Fortunately no one else on the line was gabby, although Mrs. Mundis didn't mind eavesdropping on conversations, nor did Vergie Walker.

It used to frost Mother. She'd finally say in a clear tone,

"Vergie, will you get off the line?" Naturally not a peep was heard from the ever-curious Vergie, but you did hear the faint click on the line that meant she'd hung up.

She dialed Tweetie.

"Tweetie, Juts. How are you?"

I couldn't hear what he was saying.

"I've got an able-bodied young lady here who will work for you in the mornings or after school for free in your barn. Her remuneration will be time with Suzie Q. Now, I call that a good deal. She's young and small but she's mighty." She liked to describe me like that, her mighty mouse.

Saturday at six in the morning I was dropped at Tweetie's by Dad on his way to work. Dad and his brothers owned a grocery store and meat market that had been in their family since before the Revolutionary War. When you own your own business you work all the time. He seemed to like it, though. He was a good businessman. He put people before money, which taught me you can. Because of sympathy and humor, business never slacked. He wasn't a Pollyanna but if he had to do with less to help someone eat, then he did.

Tweetie—Mr. Byrd to me—welcomed me and handed me a pitchfork. He showed me where the straw was for bedding, where to dump the manure, where to wash out the wheelbarrow, and where to put it when I was finished. He had written down in careful cursive handwriting each horse's dietary needs. He owned five horses, two pairs of matched Percherons for the plow as well as to drive, and Suzie Q, reserved only for foxhunting. Like I said, he was a successful farmer. He also owned a Brewster carriage, deep maroon with pinstripes. My God, it was a work of art, and I'd kill to own it.

He covered the packed dirt floor of the stable with cedar shavings. The aroma was so pleasant and invigorating. I had to pick out the center aisle, replace the cedar shavings, then rake the aisle.

Fortunately, the barn had electricity. He had splurged on a big water heater which was outside the work stall, enclosed in a small insulated structure. Hot water. What a luxury. The tack room was tidy, every bridle had its home, every saddle sat on its own rack. A small wood-burning stove reposed in the corner. It had been there since the early nineteenth century.

Tweetie bought oats in huge quantities and had them blown into a large outdoor corrugated zinc holder at the side of the barn. Think of it as a four-sided silo narrowing at the bottom. You flipped the latch, and out rushed the oats. He crimped them himself because it saved money. A crimp is a kind of slice or depression so the hull is split but not removed from the oat. He could have bought them crimped and steamed but it's more expensive. Crimped oats digest better, so the horses don't waste as much feed. They're just the best. Given the ease of prepared foods, people rarely use them today. As always with horsemen and equine vets, people have strong opinions. Some will argue against crimped oats. They may be right but Tweetie's horses gleamed.

"Do you know how to make a bran mash?" He looked down at me.

I felt like I was in the shadow of a mountain.

"Yes, sir. I use PopPop and G-uncle's recipe."

"And what might that be?" He had great respect for the brothers.

"You heat the water for the bran, mix it up until it's not too watery but not porridge either, throw in some flaxseed for their coat and two jiggers of cheap whiskey per horse."

"Whiskey, now?" His blue eyes twinkled.

"Yes, sir, but we don't let PopPop do the whiskey part."

Tweetie shook his head, saying nothing. My grandfather's decline saddened most people who knew him before the Great War. And of course there are always a few people who actually feel superior to the alcoholic—not many, but enough to turn your stomach. Tweetie and I both knew who they were.

Weekends, I showed up at six A.M. Sundays I would go to vespers if Mom and Dad went, or I could always go to mass with Aunt Mimi. Mother, not Catholic, didn't care if I beat my beads, as she put it. Religious dogma flew over my head. Still does.

Weekdays, I worked after school. The horses had already been fed and turned out but I picked stalls and if there was something that needed to be soaked overnight, like beet pulp, I prepared it. Beet pulp puts weight on a horse so if you have a nervous horse or one who's worked off the weight or been ill, it's a help. You have to roll up your sleeves and get your hands in it to really mix it up. On a bitterly cold day it's an onerous chore but at least the water was hot. The bucket was bigger than I was so I'd lean over, face about down in the beet pulp, to sink both arms in up to my elbows. Threw in brown sugar, just a little, and the two jiggers of whiskey per horse. Never underestimate the power of whiskey.

Even though the horses had been turned out I checked them. Picking up those big Percheron hooves, especially if the horse has a sense of humor and wants to watch you sweat, is difficult for a child.

I groomed them—such an enjoyable task, as is cleaning tack. The odor of a horse is heady perfume to me, and so is the sweet aroma of leather, oil, and saddle soap.

Once every six months I washed the tack with harsh Castile soap, stripping it. Then I'd put, say, a martingale and bridle in a bucket of light oil. Journeyman Saddlery in Middleburg makes just such an oil. After the tack had soaked a good two hours, I'd hang it up on tack hooks, a bucket under each bridle. Finally I'd wipe them dry and put them back together. Most bits, especially those made of fine English steel, were sewn in so I didn't have to worry about putting the tack back on the bridle. I cleaned the bits until they gleamed. Eventually, I reached a point where if there was a tiny pit in the steel I felt it and immediately reported it to Tweetie. He could smooth it out in his mechanic's shop. Every tool known to man and woman sat in that shop. Every tool hung on a pegboard, nothing lay on the ground.

Suzie Q repaid my efforts tenfold. We loved each other. Then again, I learned so much just being around Tweetie. He was highly organized and didn't cut corners. Eagerness must have radiated from my face, because he took me under his wing and taught me a great deal about caring for horses, and about farming, too.

Young as I was, I could ride Suzie Q. To put the bridle on I had to stand on a big box. She was patient with me and would kindly lower her head. Tweetie told me not to canter when the ground was too hard. If it was brutally hard, I wasn't to trot either. But I could always walk her up and down hills. Walking when the ground is tight saves a horse from becoming footsore. He pretended I was conditioning Suzie Q. She was in fine condition, but how thoughtful of him to make me feel competent.

Balance was all I had, since I couldn't get my legs around her big barrel. I knew nothing, but at least I could stick up there. My inner thighs ached until the muscles adjusted to the spread.

Some days it was so cold my fingers curled around the reins and didn't want to uncurl, but I didn't want to stop. Night vision isn't the problem for horses that it is for people, so on a December day at four-thirty, when the sun was setting, we could still get some riding in.

I learned diagonal leads, how to ask for a canter, how to sit a bit deep when you wanted to stop, because Suzie Q taught me. I wasn't fortunate enough to have an actual riding lesson until I was thirty-four. The way Suzie Q taught was intuitive. I could feel the changes in her rhythm with the lead. It took me awhile but I figured it out. The canter, as always, is easy. Posting creates difficulties for most people learning to ride because the tendency is to go up and down. That's not what you do. The horse's motion throws you up and down, but posting means you move your pelvis forward and backward with the motion as you rise and fall in the stirrups. It saves energy. Sitting a trot becomes tiring, especially in the hunt field. It may be easier to sit a trot in a Western saddle, but I only rode in a Western saddle once so I'm not sure. I remember it drove me crazy because I felt I had no contact with the horse. If I were on a cattle drive I bet I'd learn to appreciate it.

Suzie Q taught me to understand her language. If she lowered her head when I came to fetch her from the paddock she was interested and focused on me. If she shook her head, whether I was on foot or up on her back, that motion meant the same as it does among humans: "No," or "I don't want to do it."

Tweetie had an old McClellan saddle. Seeing me ride bareback he said I could use it, but it was just too big. Took me two weeks to reach that conclusion. I threw a square saddle pad on her with an old overgirth, a densely woven cloth girth that typically goes over the saddle. It's used in addition to the regular leather girth. You'll often see overgirths in team colors, on polo ponies. They come in different sizes and I found one that fit, even without going over a saddle. It kept the saddle pad from slipping. I'd found it while looking for something else. Isn't that always the way? I rode her bareback. I'd draw my legs up. One is supposed to reach down with the legs to get a firm grip. I couldn't do that yet. But if I kept my legs drawn up, like a jockey, I could keep my balance.

At the time I didn't think of what I was doing in these terms: a medium-sized predator making common cause with a large prey animal. We literally see the world differently. Their eyes, huge, are on the sides of their heads. Their vision is almost three hundred and sixty degrees except for a small area between the eyes. They can see you sitting up there in the saddle. Our eyes are in the center of our flat faces. We can focus intently, but we lack field of vision.

Their ears, large and movable, detect the slightest sound, and their first defense is to flee. If not, they will fight. At six years old I was starting to understand the difference between prey and predator behavior. Suzie Q knew all about how humans operate. I was the one being taught.

Draft horses have mild temperaments. If you ever have the privilege to be around a Shire, the largest of the drafts, take the opportunity to ride it. I hunted a friend's Shire once. My friend was a big man; I'm a small woman. Riding his draft horse, Oreo, made me feel like I was in a BarcaLounger. It may be a cliché, but you are in the company of a gentle giant. Belgians, a pretty breed with their golden color, are also mild. Percherons have temperament. While they are not as sensitive as Thoroughbreds, I wouldn't classify them as always mild. They have good temperaments. I like a bit of pizzazz, but not so much that I want to become airborne at regular intervals.

Suzie Q was kind. It's funny how horses recognize a child's lack of strength or ability. Rarely will a horse toss a child or someone who is not able-bodied. It does happen, but it really is unusual. Regardless of my mistakes—tugging on the reins, bringing my hands up, putting my legs in the wrong position—Suzie Q forgave me.

For the first time in my life I experienced an exhilarating partnership. We were Fred Astaire and Ginger Rogers. Horses have a big range of emotions and they sense ours. Suzie Q knew when I was peeved, hurt, happy, or tired. She'd nuzzle me if I was on the ground or put her big head over my shoulder. I'd stand on the box and run my hands along her crest. She fairly wriggled with happiness. I'd run my hands over her back and rub the muscles on either side of her spine. I'd massage her legs. We showed our affection through touch. She knew a fair number of words. The tone of my voice relayed information, but the best communicator for us was touch. Naturally, the carrots and apples helped. I liked the other horses, but I loved Suzie Q.

Some horses have a pronounced sense of humor. She sure did. If I put down my notebook and she could reach it, she'd pick it up and drop it in her stall. She'd pretend to chase the farm dogs. She'd allow the cats to walk on her back but she was very, very picky about people. If she disliked someone she avoided them or wouldn't come out of her stall corner to say hello. Literally, she showed them her ass. She didn't like nervous people or loud people. Strange, but someone can appear calm on the outside yet be churning on the inside. Horses know. Sometimes that kind of person has an "electric seat," which makes the horse hotter than a peppercorn. The horse senses this, just as they are amazingly good at identifying mental illness. Horses cannot be around crazy people. A dog or cat, depending on the type of mental illness, can often bear it, even seem to sympathize with it, but horses can't. They can deal with cerebral palsy and other forms of damage, like people without arms or legs. You can ride without your legs from the knees down, but you do need your thighs. With the advance of prosthetics, I bet there are some people who can ride with an entire manufactured leg. Horses can deal with all these conditions.

Humans' belief systems cloud reality. We think we aren't animals and we have forgotten how to read one another's bodies, much less other species'. I am speaking in broad terms but I don't think you will disagree. We are moving at warp speed away from the gifts of our species and instead are putting our faith in technology. Technology must be the servant, not the master.

Suzie Q lived into her late twenties. It was hard to leave her when we moved to the Deep South. Dad just couldn't stand the cold anymore and neither could Mother. They wanted warmth, and the vividness of deep Southern individualism. When I bade my friend goodbye, I cried. Dad, not as strict as Mother about showing one's emotions, gave me time. Tweetie gave me twenty dollars. A fortune!

Suzie Q died when I was eighteen. Mother wrote me a letter to tell me because I was in my first year at college. A wave of nostalgia and loss rolled over me. The three creatures who showed me and taught me the power of unconditional love were now gone: Dad, Chaps, and Suzie Q. Through time I learned to accept and moderate. Love surmounts even death. Love is like remembered light, it will guide you through the darkness. Suzie Q, Chaps, and Dad are still my lanterns.

A young bluejay gave me my first lesson in the rules of natural selection.
Photo courtesy of Ken Thomas at www.KenThomas.us.

Natural Selection

After years of observing and engaging in the natural world all around us, I have learned an important lesson. You can't fight nature. Calamities and death are a part of it, just as much as birth and growth are. Once you understand and accept this vast power that at times makes you feel as insignificant as a tiny particle, you can find great fulfillment in the beauty and logic of it all.

Growing up in the middle of the Appalachian chain, I had daily opportunities to marvel at the beauty of the natural world. In the spring, everything shimmered with fragrance, color, sound. There may be other parts of the world where spring and fall rival this beauty, but I've not seen them, and I've traveled a great deal, usually on business. I don't like to travel, for it takes me away from my animals.

The willows send out a hint that the change is coming with a faint cast of yellow. The crocuses are usually up by then and the snowdrops have already bloomed, literally pushing up through the snow. The robins announce their return with a characteristic "hello" chirp. Since they are just back, they chirp a lot, like old friends getting together after a long parting. They are just plain happy. Why is it so difficult for scientists to fathom that other creatures feel the joy of life? Science is always behind when it comes to the natural world. A small case in point: for years scientists taught us that dogs are color blind. A few years ago this position was reversed. Another example, in the December 19, 2008, issue of *The Manchester Guardian Weekly,* on page 45, there's a sidebar about scientists at the University of Vienna who determined that dogs get jealous. Anyone who ever lived with a dog knows this.

In spring, the redbud begins to bloom, first deep magenta, then lightening to shades of pink as buds open. Goldfinches chatter away, worse than any group of golfers at the nineteenth hole. The oaks, still barren, with rustling brown leaves still attached, might host bluejays peering down at the goldfinches wondering should they terrorize them or not. The forsythias spill cascades of yellow; as they fade, the dogwoods begin to explode. White and pink covers the whole eastern side of the Blue Ridge Mountains, which I face. The spring green glows on hickories, oaks, sycamores, and black birch, the deciduous natives of the East Coast.

I grew up in the foothills of the Appalachians. And when I was full grown, as soon as I made enough money, I repaired to the mountains themselves. Flatlanders tend to weary of our twisting roads and the fact that they can't see around corners. I often think this explains the difference between writers like Edna Ferber and William Styron. Those who live in the Rockies or the Sierra Nevada laugh at our mountains, calling them hills. Go ahead and laugh. This was once the highest mountain chain in the world. Living here forces one to comprehend the sheer power of time as well as weather. The roundness of these mountains can make a person feel like a baby leaning against his mother's breast or propped up on her thigh.

These mountains harbor life, nurture life, and take life.

My sixth spring intoxicated me. Mother loved to garden, so we were on our hands and knees putting additional loam on the beds. No mulch back then. Or if there was, we didn't know about it. We'd buy crushed seashells from the Chesapeake shores to put on the lawn and we'd buy what folks called turned dirt, a kind of light-textured loam but deep brown in color. Anything to retard the weeds, which I swear will still be here even if there's an atomic war.

Little insects ran away when I disturbed their nesting places. From time to time I'd unearth a gross fat white grub. The chickens considered them a great delicacy.

A warbler called.

Mother's head went up. "Ah, they're back."

"What?"

"Warblers. Those little birds with the big songs. Usually they're high up in the trees. I don't see them as much as I hear them. Thing is, there're lots of kinds of warblers, and their songs are similar. I have a hard time distinguishing." (Me, too.)

"Not like crows."

She smiled. "No, but people confuse bluejay calls with crows sometimes."

These were so distinct to me. "They do?"

"Honey, people don't really listen to the birds. They might like a song—a thrush, say, which is so beautiful, but they don't know it's a thrush."

"Are they stupid?" Diplomacy was a long time coming.

"No. They don't value or understand the birds." She spied a cow killer, giving it a wide berth.

A cow killer is a large ant with a vivid red velvet abdomen, the point being that their bite is so fierce it could kill a cow. In truth, it probably couldn't, but it sure hurts like hell.

A red-shouldered hawk let out a two-beat holler high up. She was over a cornfield, teeny sprouts. The lilac scent infused everything, for at the edge of the cornfield Mother had planted masses of lilacs, white, pinkish, and the beloved purple.

My enthusiasm for laying down the loam waned. I kept at it, though. Mother disdained those who started a job and didn't finish it.

We worked together in silence. When a bird called, I'd tell Mom who I thought it was. She'd correct me if I was wrong. Songs, for me anyway, are easier to identify than call notes. For one thing, they last longer.

The bluejay, tiring of inactivity, swooped down over the goldfinches, wrens, and sparrows who had left the bushes to visit Mother's birdfeeder. They flew up, made half circles, returned to the shrubs. Satisfied that he'd exercised his superiority, the bluejay busied himself on the ground, languidly picking up seeds that had shaken loose from the feeder. Full, he left. The little birds returned with a lot of noise.

Finally, job finished, we put our tools in the garden shed. Mother insisted I wear gardening gloves to protect my hands and to keep my fingernails clean. Back then a lady was supposed to have soft, well-cared-for hands. Working outside as much as we did, this proved a major challenge.

Walking toward the house from the shed I spied a baby bluejay, feathered, on the ground. I rushed to pick it up lest Tuffy, the cat, find it. Mother inspected this treasure.

"Should I climb the tree and put it back in the nest?"

"Climb up. I'll hand you the bird."

I shimmied up, which wasn't easy as the trunk was wide. At the lowest branch, I leaned down, Mother lifted up the baby. Finding the nest was easy because bluejays don't go to great pains to hide their nests. Being bold, they probably figure they can handle any crisis, which usually means a cat or even an owl eyeing those little bluejays.

Pleased with my salvation project, down I came. (Going up a tree is easier than coming down.)

The next morning I found the bird again.

Mother, at the kitchen sink, looked up when I ran in, door slamming behind me. "Don't slam the door."

"Look. Fell out again."

The little beak was open, the mouth pinkish, eyes dark. I lightly rubbed my forefinger over its head. Most animals like their heads rubbed, including humans.

"The mother pushed it out."

"Why?"

"Maybe it's sick or weak or she plain doesn't like it."

"That's cruel."

"No, it isn't. Nature is wise. We're the only animals that will keep alive those that can't fend for themselves."

"What's wrong with that?"

"Maybe not wrong, but unwise." She dried her hands on a dishtowel with a blue stripe down the middle. "Weak creatures demand care. That ties up able-bodied creatures that could be finding or producing food, that's all."

"Oh. You mean like Aunt Dooney?"

Aunt Dooney, an old lady with an ambling gait, was Big Mimi's sister. Big Mimi was Mother's and Aunt (Little) Mimi's mother. Big Mimi had many brothers and sisters, I don't know how many, but some died in infancy or quite young. Given that they were born in the 1870s and 1880s, this was not unusual. It's only in the last sixty years in the developed countries that the death of a child is seen as unusual. Aunt Dooney endured mild retardation. People didn't use to hide their mentally or physically infirm, unless they were dangerous or beyond all social intercourse. In the South, in the country, we still don't hide them. Aunt Dooney had lovely manners and was quite happy to perform regular chores. She spoke clearly, but she couldn't fathom ideas. Events she understood.

After Big Mimi died, PopPop couldn't take care of Aunt Dooney. PopPop could barely take care of himself. The two sisters, Aunt Mimi and my mother, shared her care. She'd spend a month at Aunt Mimi's, then a month with us. When Aunt Mimi's eldest daughter, Virginia Bowers, died of breast cancer at thirty-three, leaving three children behind, the boys' care fell to Aunt Mimi with help from Mom. Aunt Mimi's other daughter, Julia Ellen, named for Mom, was studying to be a nurse. She couldn't take care of Aunt Dooney. Aunt Mimi was very proud that Julia Ellen made such good grades. This was 1950, a terrible year for our family, for Ginny had inspired love from all who ever met her. She came as close to being a saint as anyone I have ever met in life.

Money was tight, too. Ken, Ginny's husband, also needed care. A strapping blond Marine, handsome as the devil, his wife's slow, agonizing death tore him apart. He fought in the front lines at Okinawa. Aggressive and tough, he became separated from his unit, facing the Japanese alone. He lived in a foxhole sitting on three rotting Japanese in that jungle heat for three days. The maggots ate on him and he was hit. It was Ken who told us how brave Ginny was. She never complained, remained cheerful, and did little chores until the very end. She died just six months after giving birth to the cutest little boy.

Mother considered my comment about Aunt Dooney. "She's useful. And if we were bluejays she could find her own seeds. I'm talking about animals that just can't survive on their own. We'll keep them alive, and if you think about it, everyone suffers."

"Because they'll never get better?"

"Pretty much. It's a terrible thing to be useless. Bad enough to be weak and sick, but to be useless is the worst thing that can happen to a person."

Having heard, countless times, "Idle hands do the Devil's work," I finally started to understand what it meant.

"Well, I'm going to try to keep this little guy alive."

I took one of Mother's shoeboxes, put in some fennel seeds and other little seeds from Mother's stockpile. I also put in a little saucer of water, but I gave the bluejay a drink from an eyedropper. It did drink. I put the shoebox in my bedroom window for light and closed the door since the cats would have dispatched him.

Mother came to my bedroom each night before I went to sleep. Dad was at work but if he ever got home early, he did, too. Old as I am, I miss that. I miss someone sitting on the edge of the bed telling stories, recounting the day, or just seeing to my well-being.

She walked over to the window and peeped in at the little peeper. "Honey, in the morning he'll be dead, but you've done all you can."

"Oh, Mom." I refused to cry.

Crying or displaying too much emotion figured into many a lecture, since all too often I displayed my temper.

Early the next morning I hopped out of bed. Sure enough, the bluejay had gone to the Great Bluejay in the Sky. Blasting down the stairway to the kitchen, I found Mother putting on a pot of water. I loved tea, we all did. A glass of orange juice sat on the table.

"Would you like to bury your bird?"

She'd come into my room while I was sleeping, something she often did, so she knew about the bluejay.

"Okay."

After breakfast (which I had no appetite for), I carried the shoebox up to the crabapple tree and there we planted Birdie. I recited the Twenty-third Psalm, my favorite.

Mother walked back with me. How she could keep a straight face I don't know, except that she did love animals and my childish attempt at ritual was accepted.

"You can cry sometimes. Some occasions."

"Nah. He was a little bird and I didn't know him too well."

She laughed. "You're a bird, a catbird."

Being a catbird in the South is a compliment.

I felt instantly better.

Nature not only abhors a vacuum, she abhors waste. A creature that can't fend for itself is wasteful. Animals have litters, culling out those that can't survive. Humans, centuries ago, also culled. Often if there was little money they'd get rid of the girl babies. The ancient Greeks practiced this. The Greeks gave it up but we all know other cultures do this, usually aborting the female fetus. There will be hell to pay when males outnumber females and they reach breeding age. Of course, Europeans and those in the Americas don't do this anymore. Given modern medicine, many newborns survive that couldn't have even twenty years ago. This is a blessing until you start thinking about the dangers of overpopulation.

Later day that, back at the loam, Mother said, "It's a funny thing. I was thinking about Birdie. His mother knew. I said to you maybe his mother didn't like him. I was joking, but you know, I started to think about that. A human being who can't get along is another kind of burden. There are those who are violent, those who are bad crazy, not good crazy. But even those who lack all social skills are a burden. You have to continually repair the fences they've broken. Next time you complain about your tea lessons, remember that." (Tea lessons were pre-cotillions. Learning manners in the South starts before kindergarten. The formal training ends, at least for us, with a huge Christmas ball in the year one turns eighteen.

"But, Mom, you tell me to take people as I find them. That means even the ones that will tell a lady she's fat."

"Me and my big mouth." She put down her trowel. "I don't know, I'm just thinking about people who don't fit in. I don't mean we're supposed to be alike. That would bore me to death. But I truly believe we're all capable of exhibiting good manners. Birdie just got me thinking."

Me, too.

Walking out the bassets.

Animals Bring Out the Best in Us

You've probably driven down a road at least once in your life and noticed a skinny man walking. He's lost his driver's license due to drinking. If he's thirty, he looks fifty. Booze lacerates looks. That was George Harmon, my PopPop.

Born 1888, my grandfather suffered in the trenches of World War I. Those who knew him before the Great War said he wasn't a drunk. He held a job as a skilled carpenter and he was fun. After the war he retained his skills but not his reliability. Foxhounds saved him.

As long as Big Mimi was alive he managed to bring in a little money. Big Mimi, Mother's mother, was his wife. She died on February 6, 1948. As I was born November 28, 1944, I remember some of those times firsthand, but not much. I do remember that PopPop fell apart at the funeral. He sobbed so hard it took two men, Dad and PopPop's brother, Bob Harmon, to hold him up.

He drank nonstop after that. Mother and Aunt Mimi called on him almost daily. They lived in York and Hanover, Pennsylvania, right over the Mason–Dixon Line. PopPop lived on a farm in Spring Grove and Bob Harmon lived in one of the tight little houses at Green Spring Valley Hunt Club in Maryland. Bad roads ate up great chunks of driving time but the family kept visiting. They were afraid PopPop would kill himself. He couldn't work. No one would hire him, with good reason.

Bob couldn't get PopPop a job at the hunt club, even though PopPop was a good hand with hounds and not bad with horses. Redmond Stewart, MFH (Master of Foxhounds), founded Green Spring Valley Hunt, which is usually referred to as GVH. He had more money than God and was also a World War I vet but he entered the war as an officer. I think he was a lawyer, and he was already in his forties when war broke out. Mr. Stewart was Over There but he never saw combat. G-uncle Bob said his commanding officer allowed Redmond to lead a line of men up to the front but made him return. Both Bob and PopPop always suspected that Redmond felt both guilt and anger that he didn't get a chance to fight. After the war, Redmond returned to his lucrative life in Baltimore and single-handedly supported GVH, guiding it toward the enviable reputation it enjoys to this day. If you hunt with GVH, you really hunt.

But while Redmond was cheap when it came to spending or giving away money, according to G-uncle Bob, he could be generous in other ways. He felt particularly close to men who had fought, and he knew PopPop. Redmond and Bob figured that one way to keep PopPop alive would be to retire hounds to him so he could enter contests with them.

PopPop built nice runs and big lodges, and happily took two couples (four hounds—hounds have been measured in couples since the days of the Pharaohs). They wouldn't give him more because they knew he had little money. He'd starve to feed his hounds. My family's like that. I've gone hungry myself (no one knew) but my horses and hounds gleamed. Learned that from my afflicted grandfather. If you assume the responsibility for a child or an animal, they always come first.

He began competing in hunting contests. A number is painted on a hound's hip. They are all released at the same time and the first one to put his fox to ground wins. For coon hunters, their hound must tree the coon. Officials judging the competition follow the action on horseback or in a truck, depending on the venue. Pop-Pop's gift with hounds served him well. He'd win pretty often and get ten dollars. The big hunts had prizes of fifty dollars plus lots of dog food. Fifty dollars back then would be a whole lot of money now.

Redmond died before I was born. I regret not knowing him because those who did spoke highly of him. G-uncle Bob stayed on at GVH and PopPop received hounds whenever he needed them. He got the ones with the best noses who retained some speed but were now a step slow for GVH, which is a blazingly fast hunt.

No booze before a contest. By the time I came into his life he was a wiry man, gray hair in a buzz cut, the face of a confirmed alcoholic. Broken veins, deep creases, and sallow skin made him look a lot older than his sixty-some years. He walked everywhere or rode an old black Schwinn bicycle, so his body looked a lot better than his face. Everyone on the Harmon, Huff, Zepp, Finster, Buckingham side of the family is good with machines, especially the women. For a guy, PopPop did okay. But if something really broke down, Mother and Aunt Mimi would come and fix it. They could fix trucks and tractors, so bicycles were a snap. Back then, riding a bicycle wasn't necessarily an admission of alcoholism. Even with Ford's mass production revolution, motor vehicles, whether trucks, cars, or boats, remained out of reach for many. But PopPop needed his bike, swore he wouldn't pedal it drunk. Usually he kept that promise but sometimes he'd fall over in a ditch only to wake up wet and muddy, hauled home by a friend.

I showed a flair for hounds very early. This thrilled my grandfather. He promised Mother if I stayed with him sometimes, he wouldn't drink. He didn't. When I look back I wonder what that cost him. Sometimes he'd shake, his hands just trembling like leaves in the wind, but he never complained and he didn't cheat on his promise. He had a Marylander's pride and he never wanted me to see him in that deplorable condition where he'd get so bad he'd mess himself.

Sometimes Mother and Aunt Mimi would find him and need to clean him up. I think even today there are people who care for their blood or friends that way, but most, if they have any money at all, pack them off to rehab. No rehab then. Not that we knew about.

Mother always said that even falling-down drunk, PopPop fed, watered, and cleaned his hounds.

He taught me to put bag balm on their paw pads if they became footsore. He showed me, after a cow or sheep was rendered, how to cook up a meat and barley stew for them. Start with a little flaxseed or corn, toss in a touch of cheap bourbon or whiskey. I've never seen hounds since to match PopPop's hounds.

I'm trying to build an addition onto my kennels so that I can have a block and tackle, a walk-in freezer, and one of those huge iron pots that take four men to move so I can duplicate PopPop's recipe. Until then, it's commercial kibble, which is good, but what could be better than warm gruel on a cold day after you've run fifty miles?

Conditioning and nutrition are critical. Teaching me gave PopPop a lift to his step. He wasn't talkative. He'd tell me what I needed to know, like, "Buzz, cook until the meat falls off the bones. Dry the bones out. Save them, let them dry out, and then grind them up." He'd pour into the gruel the ground bones from, say, last week's cooking. "Use barley. Don't use wheat. If you can get rice, that's good, but we can't get it here as easily as barley, which is all around. Put in this much flaxseed." He'd pour in two gallons (the pot could hold two grown men). "Corn oil is good but expensive. If you become a rich woman, use corn oil." He'd wink. "Course you could marry a rich man, but don't marry him if he's not a foxhunter." A deep breath. "Or at least some kind of hunter. A man that doesn't hunt isn't a man." I never disputed this and don't much to this day, although I realize for many, hunting opportunities are slipping. Then there are those who demonize all hunters, portraying them as bloodthirsty dolts.

On these lessons would go. Usually I kept my trap shut. Sometimes I'd ask a question. Training fascinated me. He'd go into a run with puppies, eight weeks old. "All they need to know is their name." He'd call a puppy's name and if they came, he'd give them a little treat. He played games with them, which encouraged hunting prowess. To this day, I still use some of those games with my own pups.

The most important things he taught me were:

Love your hounds.

Trust your hounds. If you can't trust a hound, don't hunt him.

If anyone mistreats your hound, never speak to them again. If they hurt a hound, bide your time but hurt them back.

Now, that might sound ugly, but people are pack animals. Let one misbehave, and the pack begins to disintegrate. If you don't establish your position, people will walk all over you. If you have to hurt them, hurt them. He never told me how to hurt them, but over the years I learned a variety of ways to get even with anyone who misread my cotillion manners for weakness and to really smash anyone who hurt a hound, a horse, a cat, or a fox.

People that hurt animals will eventually hurt people. You can't tolerate it. The law allows what honor forbids. Besides, in my experience, the law only belongs to those who can afford it.

I'd go with him to contests. Dad drove. Frost sparkled on cornstalks. What excitement. Men would pay an entry fee per hound, usually two dollars but sometimes as much as five, which was a lot of money. You could eat for a week for five dollars. The hounds got a number painted on each hindquarter. The judges mounted up, usually on quiet horses since some of the judges couldn't have gotten back on if they fell off. Too much pie. Wives, girlfriends came along but I didn't see women hunting the hounds. We all knew some of them worked in the kennels, but back then you made the man look good even if he wasn't. If the ladies resented it, I didn't know, but I was too little to know. I sure resented it as I grew.

Two incidents from those hunts are vivid and still guide me today. One I wrote about in *Rita Will*. As PopPop deteriorated further he started to cheat. I unwittingly helped. He'd go to the cast (where you'd first let out your hound or hounds) with a gorgeous hound who ran silent. We'd go in the middle of the night. We'd follow on foot as best we could to learn where the foxes were and where the freshest scent was up to that time. Then we'd come back the next morning and he'd release the hounds that spoke. If the hunt was way far from his little house we couldn't do this since he couldn't drive.

I told Mother once I realized what was going on. She said, "Keep it to yourself. Sometimes people have to break the rules to live. He's suffered in this life." So I never told until I wrote *Rita Will* because they're all gone now.

There are people who break other people for the sake of obeying the rules, and there are people who break the rules to help others. I hope, thanks to Mother and Dad, I fall into the latter category. Not that I'm looking to cheat, but I figure you could throw out ninety percent of all federal, state, and county legislation and we'd all be happier, and far, far more productive.

The other lesson I learned involved a German baker. He'd been successful, eventually selling his store and recipes to a larger company. He'd fled the rise of the Nazis, and he was a decorated World War I vet. He grew up with a different kind of hound than we had, but he enjoyed working with hounds. So he got himself some American foxhounds and started learning about them and vice versa.

I mention American because here there are four kinds of foxhounds: English, American, Crossbred (a combination of the two), and Penn-marydels. Each has its virtues. I prefer the American, most especially Bywaters Blood or Skinker Blood (Orange County) hounds from The Plains, Virginia.

PopPop and Hans (PopPop called him Johnny) met at a hound trial. Typical of hound people, they started trading stories and tips. PopPop helped Hans a lot because Hans wanted a system. American hounds, like Thoroughbred horses, are terribly sensitive, though often very affectionate. Not everyone can or should handle them.

"No system." PopPop would shake his head. "Each hound is a snowflake."

Hans struggled with this. He'd been in the German army, after all, and rules and orders were the breath of life. Systems tend to be a German trait. I base this observation on my numerous visits there, and let me be clear: I really adore Germany, and I'm partial to Austria, too. But PopPop kept telling Hans he had to relax, be flexible, let the hound tell him what it would do and how quickly it would learn. He used a horseman's term: "Don't run him through the bridle."

Since these men were born before automobiles, Hans got it. His English, heavily accented, a northern accent, was very good. He was a fine man with a booming sense of humor who always fussed over me. Naturally, I adored him, and his wife, too.

Hans worked tirelessly with his American hounds. He began to win. He won a big one, walking off with fifty dollars. The first person to shake his hand was my grandfather, who really could have used that prize money.

When PopPop, Dad, and our two hounds, Buster and Bromo, loaded up in the car, we found an envelope on the driver's seat written in the most beautiful script I ever had seen. It was addressed to Herr George Harmon and Buster and Bromo. The paper was watermarked. I noticed signs of elegance like that, even then, because Mother pounded it into me.

The letter simply read, "Corporal Harmon: Thank you. Sergeant Haxthausen."

PopPop, much as he needed the money, struggled, for the gift was so large. Dad finally stepped in. "George, to return or refuse a gift is an insult pretty much anywhere in the world. Go thank him."

PopPop's eyes got glassy. He folded the letter and I watched him walk to where Hans was receiving congratulations, along with his wife. Well, she was so pretty, the men just wanted to touch her, so they shook her hand, too.

I tagged along at a distance but Dad held me back from joining the crowd. PopPop shook Hans's hand and I heard him say, "Thank you, Johnny."

Then Hans, happy as he could be, loudly proclaimed, "Taught

me how to deal with an American hound. I just got lucky today."
He paused. "To think we nearly killed one another." Everyone
laughed.

"Daddy, why are they laughing?"

He squeezed my hand. "They were within a hundred yards or
so of each other in the trenches."

This troubled me. "Does that mean Johnny is our enemy?"

"No, honey. Old men start wars, young men fight them. It's
ugly." Dad, in the Civil Air Patrol, escaped combat, not by his
choice.

A few years later Hans died in an auto accident. PopPop went
to the funeral in his uniform. When they lowered the casket he
saluted. He cried, everyone cried. A good man is a good man in
any country, any time.

That was an important lesson for me, but just as important
was seeing how animals brought people together. What healers
they are as well as best friends. Foxhounds truly saved my grandfather.

PopPop finally died in the mid-1950s. There was hardly anything of him left. His friends who competed against him knew the
value of his hounds. They gave Mother and Aunt Mimi money
for them, which upset me as I swore I could hunt them. No one
derided me, but it wasn't in the cards at that time.

Beauty, the hound who ran silent, came to me and she lived
with Chaps, who loved having a friend. What I know of hounds
and hunting I credit to PopPop, G-uncle Bob, and Beauty, and to
the fact that love never dies. Those hounds I followed, the puppies he taught while I watched, PopPop himself, they each loved
me in their way. I'm sending it along.

Chickens stick to their pecking order even more strictly than humans.
Photo by Judy Pastore.

The Pecking Order

Ever notice how there's always a low man on the totem pole no matter what the group is? Herd and pack animals create hierarchies. Cats don't, since every cat is the king or queen of all he or she surveys. Why hierarchies are so important I don't know. I never will. On the one hand, they create stability. On the other hand, they engender suffering. The worst thing you can do to a pack animal is to remove it from the pack. Even being the bottom man isn't as painful. No wonder solitary confinement is perceived as the worst punishment for a human, short of torture and death.

Chickens stick to their pecking order even more strictly than humans. A human has the possibility to rise through effort. A chicken doesn't, until some of the higher chickens die. Then the bird can move up the ladder. But some birds, just like people, are so peculiar or outlandish to other members of their species that they can't be borne.

Except for those times of purgatory when I had to live in cities to acquire my higher miseducation (the Greek and Latin were worth it) and to establish my career, I've kept chickens. When I was quite small, I fed them. In our family, as soon as you could walk, you were taught to perform service. You didn't work, you didn't eat. It only took being sent to bed a couple of times without supper to end laziness. Pride grows when you see your chores help the family.

Our chickens were Rhode Island Reds, Leghorns, and Plymouth Barred Rock. When I entered the pen they'd rush up to me. The cats reposed outside the pen, dreaming of the day when one, just one, chicken would escape. The dogs, bored stiff by the cackling, showed little interest.

One big white chicken, a Leghorn, was literally henpecked. She had no feathers on her back. Much as I felt sorry for her, she managed. One other chicken was ostracized from the group completely. I'd throw her cracked corn as far as I could, after putting out a big pile for the others, so she could eat in peace. She lived under the chicken house because the others drove her from it. I asked Mother if I should find her a pen of her own and Mother replied that the chicken would rather be near her own kind even though they mistreated her.

Feathers decorated hats then. The more exotic the feather, the more expensive the hat. All ladies and gentlemen wore hats. Everyone looked attractive. You acquire a sense of personality when you're sporting a hat. Different hats were suitable for different occasions.

Didn't matter if you dressed up to go to town or you bumped along on your Johnny Pop (a John Deere tractor that made a pop from the exhaust), your work hat or everyday hat became your signature.

Dress-up hats, church hats, and rain hats contributed to your turnout, but your work hat really was you. Mother's work hat was a soft straw hat, wide brim, black grosgrain ribbon. She gardened in it, went to market in it. Sometimes in winter she wore a navy blue fedora.

One lady in Mother's group of friends, Agnes, sported the best hats. She had pheasant feathers for sporting occasions, feathers I couldn't identify but that were dyed for other social occasions. She favored capes, too. As she was statuesque and a registered redhead, every man in the county was in love with her except her husband. She craved affection and found it easily. When the wives of the men supplying the much-needed emotional attention discovered their husbands' generosity, Agnes found herself the subject of sulphurous reaction. What fascinated me as a child was that the wives nine times out of ten put the husband on their reserve shit list, while Agnes topped it. Agnes didn't take a vow to be faithful to their marriage, though the husbands sure did. Agnes wasn't often invited to parties. She wasn't completely ostracized, but she was often pushed outside the circle.

Mother liked her. The woman had a great sense of humor as well as style. And she wasn't the first woman to look for love in all the wrong places. Divorce was a horrendous stain then. Better to be in a miserable marriage than no marriage at all. Her solution to the desiccation of her emotional life seemed better than no solution at all.

Around this time, when I was about seven, I noticed that many women drank secretly. It was one of many things I had observed in the adult world that mystified me.

The chickens lacked recourse to sippin' whiskey. Their pleasure was their feed, hence plumpness. Some people take that route, too.

One of Agnes's worst critics, Deirdre, was an engine of exclusiveness, forever stirring up other women. She'd make her bid at the bridge table and then casually look at her opponent and say, "Anne, saw Hoppy chatting up Agnes down at the filling station today. He checked her tire pressure before the grease monkey could get to it." As Hoppy was Anne's husband, this produced the desired effect.

Mother loathed this. Aunt Mimi learned to listen but she swore she didn't like it either. Mother could turn away from gossip, cutting the person short. Sis had to hear the whole story, slapping on her moral cosmetics.

One day Mother and I walked through the town square as Agnes approached from the opposite direction. The two women waved, and when they reached each other, they noted the weather, the standard conversation opener in our parts. Then they moved on to events, politics, upcoming holidays. Agnes's hat, green, resembled a Borsalino. A wide same-colored grosgrain ribbon banded it with a quarter-moon pinned on the side of the ribbon, badger fur protruding. A mass of pheasant feathers with a few red feathers interspersed provided a vivid backdrop for the groomed tufts of badger fur. I coveted that hat. Mother wore a simple slouch, I wore a lad's cap. I still wear them, as they keep your head warm and they're so comfortable.

Sure enough, sailing around the Square like an outrigger in a high wind, Deirdre approached. Her hat, broad-brimmed with cascades of ostrich feathers in electric purple, bounced as she clipped along. All she needed was a mainsail.

As she passed she called hello to Mother while snubbing Agnes. Agnes's face turned red.

Mother said, "Agnes, don't go out of your way to piss on a skunk."

Agnes laughed, and that was that.

Later Aunt Mimi stopped by. The two sisters rarely passed a day without at least one visit, usually two.

Mother said, "Sis, saw Deirdre on the Square and she appears to have recovered from her recent bout of good health. I was talking to Agnes and Deirdre snubbed her. I know it was Deirdre even though I could barely see her face for the feathers on her hat—screaming purple, mind you."

Aunt Mimi perked up, "What kind of feathers?"

"Vulture."

Agnes persevered. As she aged and opportunities for outside affection waned, she accepted her lot. Like most women she needed her husband's money to survive. A middle-class or working-class woman who could manage to get herself an education might become a nurse, a schoolteacher, or a secretary. But the wages were pitifully low. Small wonder divorce wasn't an option. Agnes's looks held up and she let her hair turn a beautiful silver. Little by little she moved further into the circle.

Deirdre's fulminations became tedious and she began to lose her position. She wasn't shut out, but she wasn't embraced either. Meanwhile, Mother, welcoming to most, kept her iron lock on the county. She deserved it. She was a natural leader.

My chicken, unloved except by me, hung in there, too. She lived a long life, always on the outskirts, still under the chicken house where she'd burrowed herself a deep hole. When the first frost came, around October 15, I'd lie flat on my belly and crawl under the coop to fill her hole with straw. Maybe she lived so long because she was hardened to the elements. Some of the other chickens, committing offenses unknown to me, were pecked to death over the years.

None of the ladies in Mother's circle pecked one another to death, despite their fine feathers.

Today I have my chickens. There's a serial killer in my coop. She hops into other nests to peck open the eggs. She eludes me.

I think I know who it is and yet I'm not sure. I didn't encounter this as a child. Surely my chickens know who this is. So far they've done nothing.

I've never caught a chicken thieving, but other birds certainly do it, and dogs are expert at it.

Cowbirds, on the other hand, aren't much for stealing, but they'll lay an egg in another bird's nest, thereby avoiding paying college tuition. Think this strategy would work for us?

Me at three, with Aunt Mimi's Rags.

Love Restores

A cloud of disgrace hovered over me. I'd put goldfish in the baptismal font. Since God created the world and all the flora and fauna within, I felt the beautiful Georgian church where our family had worshipped since 1622 should host life. Originally the church was a log cabin. As the colony boomed, religious architecture followed suit.

A call from the sexton alerted Mother to my deed. Down the steep hill she roared, full accelerator, the only way Mother drove. Back came Mom, back came the goldfish. I was grounded for a week. Sacrilege was the verdict.

This was much worse than the time I threw Baby Ruths into a distant neighbor's fancy swimming pool and a rumor circulated that my Aunt Mimi had pooped in the water. On that occasion Mother had affected horror and Aunt Mimi had pitched a fit. But even at the age of eight, I knew that this goldfish incident was far more serious.

I knew what sacrilege meant: no freedoms, no pay for my farm chores. City kids were given an allowance, and maybe they earned it. But in the country, we only received our fifty cents or a dollar (a practice that usually began by the age of ten) when our chores had been completed to satisfaction. "Satisfaction" meant some adult checked your efforts. Correction came swiftly but wasn't necessarily ugly. We were expected to do a job and do it right. If you heard the word "half-assed," you knew you'd have to start all over again.

Sacrilege was much worse than half-assed. I'd figured this out months ago when my cousin flipped the bird at another acolyte and Aunt Mimi blew up like Mount Vesuvius.

Both sisters possessed strong faith, a gift they bequeathed to me. However, Aunt Mimi was far too enraptured with church dogma. Added to this was her tendency to always want to be right. If you're spouting the Word of God how can you be wrong? She was Catholic. Mother and Dad came from different religious backgrounds so they compromised by being Lutheran (Episcopal in a pinch). Aunt Mimi reproved them regularly as to their grievous error.

When you entered Aunt Mimi's home, decorated to a T, you were in danger of decapitation or at least eye-gouging from low-hanging rosary beads. Then, too, she'd show you her autographed copy of the New Testament. At least, that's what Mother would joke about, behind her big sister's back. Mother'd be sitting at the kitchen table, Chesterfield blazing, coffee steaming in the cup, taking a much-needed break with one of her many pals. When all other ideas for frolic failed, they'd laugh about riding over the hill to witness Jesus' signature. This is one joke I actually believe everyone kept from my far-too-religious aunt.

So I knew that when the word "sacrilege" reached her bejeweled ears, there would be hell to pay. There was, in the form of a lecture about the sacrament of baptism, followed by a sermon about proper deportment for a lady of a certain background. The very act of putting goldfish in the baptismal font would someday obliterate my chances for a suitable marriage. She may have had a point there, for I have yet to acquire a suitable husband or wife.

(For those of you who think you know something about me, you probably don't. I've fought for better treatment and rights for many groups including gay people. I'm not the least bit put off to be called gay. In fact, I take it as a compliment. However, I have a whimsical disregard for gender.)

Anyway, the thunder rolled. Shame on me. Actually, it rolled right over me because I didn't give a fig. The barb that harpooned me was a blunt pronouncement from both sisters. They leveled their lustrous gray eyes at me, the electric silver streaks in their hair already prominent off to the left side of their widow's peaks, and said in unison, "That was a cruel thing you did."

"I put them in water."

"That water doesn't have bubbles. They would have suffocated." Aunt Mimi sniffed.

As far as I knew she didn't care much for fish except on Fridays.

"People dip their hands in the water." Mother sucked down a lungful of smoke. "Dirt's not good, you know." Then she burst out laughing. "Wouldn't you have killed to see Boody Caswell stick her fingers in there to make the sign of the cross and see four goldfish?"

"Think she'd have screamed, or passed out?" Aunt Mimi tried not to laugh, correctly gauging that this would lessen my shame.

"Scream first, then hit the floor." Mother giggled.

"Oh, Juts. She'd break a floor joist."

They could contain it no longer, for Boody was humongously fat.

However, I felt bad. I wouldn't choose to hurt any animal unless it was wild and charging me or in pain and dangerous. I'd seen animal cruelty. Well, I'd seen people cruelty, too, but animal cruelty affected me more. Unless directed at children too young to grasp just why they were on the short end of the stick, at least humans knew why they were being pummeled, even if the act was wrong.

That summer three boys from neighboring farms caught a garter snake and fried it—while it was still alive—in a tin can. I hated them for it. Might be a snake but it didn't do anything to them. Plus Mother said snakes are a farmer's friend, especially a blacksnake in the hayloft. Snakes usually get out of your way, and while four of the five poisonous snakes in North America reside in my state, they really do slither away.

Whenever I visited PopPop Harmon I would pass a man who kept a brace (a pair) of beagles. They were chained up and living in filth. Covered in sores, filled with parasites, their ribs sticking out. I'd stop and throw them the sandwich Mother had made for me, dividing it in two. They wagged their tails at me.

One fall afternoon, a Friday, I was allowed to go visit PopPop. Aunt Mimi ran me over to his little farm. All his foxhounds got along with his cats (mine, too), and one of the big ginger cats was sleeping on a chair with his four paws tucked under him.

"Means cold weather ahead," PopPop said.

Sure enough, that night a cold front came in, the wind rattling the farmhouse.

The next morning we took the foxhounds out to hunt on foot, passing the beagles, who were shivering. They had no doghouses and not enough fat to warm them.

Later, sound carrying that evening, we heard PopPop's neighbor cuss them and heard them cry out. Tears ran down my cheeks. PopPop said nothing, but he awakened me in the middle of the night. We crept over to the neighbor's house, PopPop armed with heavy bolt cutters. He cut the chains, and the little things were so weak we had to carry them back to his house. The first thing he did was feed them some warm gruel. Then we set to bathing them and toweling them off. We fluffed up an old blanket in the corner, where they gratefully slept.

The next morning PopPop wormed them, which was a mess because we couldn't let them out lest the owner see or hear them. As it was, we needed to hide them and get them out of there as soon as possible.

"Dad will help."

"I know he will." PopPop smiled.

As far as we knew, the owner hadn't searched for them, but he was capable of being as big a drunk as PopPop was, so maybe he was still sleeping.

Dad arrived and put PopPop's old blanket in the back of the car, along with me and the two beagles. When we got them home, Mother, who didn't like dogs in the house (she changed her mind later), fussed for all of three minutes and then set to work. More food. Grooming.

Tuffy, the tiger cat (Mickey had passed away by now), huffed with disapproval. Within a month the two hounds sported shiny coats, bright eyes, and happy temperaments.

How could they forgive humans? Since then I have worked with many abused animals. As I write, there are four on the farm that wandered in or were dumped here.

A tricolor Walker hound, starved and beat up, growled if any-one came near. Finally, I managed to get him to come home with me by opening a can of dog food. He followed the delicious odor and he did come into the house. Took two of us to get him to the vet for shots and a checkup. He wasn't a nasty dog, but he'd growl if I got too close. He liked it when I talked to him, and if I left a toy on the floor, he would come pick it up. What a beautiful dog he was, wonderful conformation. Eventually, he'd follow me wherever I went. He'd trot along when I worked the horses, and if I opened the door of the truck, he'd hop in, but he still didn't want to be touched. I never stared him down. I'd look at him sideways and I spoke in a soft, low tone.

I called him Bruno. Smart, smart, smart, he learned his name in a day. Like most hounds he was fanatically clean. If only I could get them to do my housekeeping.

This went on for two years. One day I walked up from the barn with Bruno beside me. I stopped because my deep pink rosebush by the back of the house had burst into splendor. He put his head under my hand. After that I could pet him, groom him, and sing to him. For whatever reason, he liked this, and I've since given each of my dogs a special song. They love it.

Bruno and I were inseparable. He lived eleven years after I found him, and I expect he was two or three then. One day he looked a little off, and the next day, too. Took him to the vet and discovered he was going into renal failure, a condition that seems to be prevalent in big hounds. I brought him home. A friend who is our equine vet was coming to the farm that day, so he died at home. I hate to put an animal down at the vet's. They're already scared.

Bruno left this earth surrounded by love. I miss him terribly. Not only was he my shadow, but that dog would have died to protect me. Once he gave me his heart he held nothing back. And maybe I loved him so much because the path to friendship took such a long time.

So often people misperceive a dog, or a horse, as vicious when what they are is frightened or deeply mistrustful. Be patient.

It won't take too long to ascertain whether an animal is really vicious. I've met very few mean dogs and only one truly nasty horse.

You've heard it a million times, but hear it once more: love works miracles.

The beagles, Charlie and Cappy, taught me how love restores. They also taught me a bit about rabbit hunting, although I claim no deep knowledge there.

Charlie and Cappy showed me that, for me, deep happiness comes from saving a dog, a cat, the occasional horse, even a cow. I'm not revealing this to make you believe how good I am. I don't do it for anyone's good opinion except my own. Anything I have done for animals has been repaid a thousandfold.

Usually I can find the animal a home when it's ready. Those that are too ugly and those that require too much maintenance to live anywhere else usually wind up on my couch.

PopPop taught me so much, but this lesson was crucial: do what you must when you must. No one in our family sets much store by laws. When you see a creature in distress you can call Animal Control. Usually they come out. During hard economic times those people are so overwhelmed, and, I might add, underpaid. People abandon children during hard times. Animals they cast aside like Dixie cups. Act. This was pressed upon me over and over again in a variety of forms: Act. Don't tell anyone what you're doing. Don't call the authorities unless the problem really is too big for you to handle.

Our motto was "No man's property or life is safe when Congress is in session." This applies to animals, too. The laws against animal cruelty may seem sensible, but usually they aren't. Again, these are attempts by people as sickened as I am but who aren't country (for lack of a better description). Their efforts often do as much harm as good, particularly when those efforts take legislative form.

If you play by the rules, first, you must prove neglect or cruelty in court. Get out your checkbook. Second, the accused now sees your face. And some of these people are only too happy to pass on their cruelty to you, maybe by burning down your barn with the horses in it. If you live at East Sixty-seventh Street and Third Avenue in Manhattan this has probably not occurred to you. But where I live, it's all too plausible.

Taking action on your own solves the problem, hopefully, for that one abused animal, but it doesn't fix the overall problem. Ours is an overregulated country with pockets of freedom. Anyone can breed even if they can't feed their children. Fine. Just don't ask me to feed them. Anyone can have animals, too, and not take care of them until discovered.

It's funny, we interfere in an individual's ability to earn a living, hogtie them with regulations, punish them with taxes, which are then grotesquely squandered. The more productive the person, the greater the punishment. Yet we allow brutality to roll along with nary a slap on the wrist: witness the still ongoing struggle over rape prevention.

Is it me or does this seem insane to you, too?

Again, I have learned to act with disregard for the law. I will continue to do so. I will call upon our sheriff (we are well served in Nelson County by our law enforcement people and by Animal Control and the Almost Home Shelter) if I need to. Otherwise, I go about my business. Our public servants in Nelson County are on overload. If I can spare them one more thing to do, I will. As an aside, the people that work in the courthouse in Lovingston are so helpful, plus everyone there has a slightly cracked sense of humor.

You and I will not solve animal cruelty, child abuse, wife beating, rape, or murders based on gender. We can lessen it, though.

I thank Charlie and Cappy for showing me I can do something useful in this life. I also thank them for teaching me that hunting a prey animal is different than hunting a predator. Down those two noses would go; the bunny would sit tight, since stillness is a major defense for prey. Speedy flight is the backup. How we'd work to flush our game, and off would go the bunny, zigging and zagging with two much-loved beagles in hot pursuit giving tongue. No, beagle voices don't sound like the bells of Moscow, but a hound giving tongue is a peal of Mozart to me. What joy. What a thrill to be working together with another species for a common goal.

By the bye, the brutal original owner of Charlie and Cappy died the following spring. He'd been dead awhile when one of the other farmers found him, drawn to his home by the terrible stink. When the ambulance came to pick up the body, his arms and legs came off. PopPop had seen enough of this in the Great War. When he heard about it he shrugged.

What kind of life must it have been for no one to claim the body, no one to grieve, no one to even say a prayer? Charlie and Cappy certainly never grieved.

PopPop said, "One less to worry about." That was that.

The other thing I learned from this was the power of a little girl's tears. My grandfather, upset though he was, did nothing to help those sad little dogs until I cried. My distress brought out the best in him, and Charlie and Cappy brought out the best in me.

As to the goldfish, they lived as long as little goldfish do, with a mermaid laid in their tank, the tiny bubbles spiraling upwards, the fake seaweed waving slightly. To this day I can never see a goldfish without wanting to make the sign of the cross.

Local steeplechase races still give me a thrill. *Photo by Danielle A. Durkin.*

When I was growing up, racetracks dotted the Mid-Atlantic landscape. Big Thoroughbred stables trained horses on their own tracks. County fairs cleaned up their tracks for harness racing, and state fairs usually boasted excellent tracks as well. Standardbreds were as popular as Thoroughbreds. The big wonderful tracks like Pimlico and Belmont topped the high end for Thoroughbreds, but many tracks filled the niches in between, right down to the end-of-the-line tracks, which made me sad as a child and continue to do so.

Harness racing touched everyone then. Flat racing (middle distance racing on flat terrain) and steeplechasing (longer distance racing with hurdles like fences and ditches) excited us all. But just about everyone, at least where I was raised, knew someone with a sulky, a light cart on two wheels with a single seat for the driver. A sulky is what you'd drive for harness racing. Driving in fine harness still held considerable social cachet. Today, many people have ridden a horse at least once in their lives. The ones who suffered a bad experience are quick to relate it, swearing they'll never do that again. Pity. Would you stop playing baseball if you got beaned?

But baseball is human versus human. Riding or driving is a human and horse partnership. Most people don't know how to communicate with a horse. I'm not saying that everyone understood horses when I was a kid, but they enjoyed a much greater familiarity with them.

Mother, who had a fabulous eye for a horse, was born in 1905. When she was born, roughly ninety percent of Americans lived in the country, ten percent in the cities. I was born at the end of 1944, and the ratio then was near to fifty-fifty. Today, ninety percent live in cities or suburbs and only ten percent of us dwell in the country. Country knowledge is shrinking. The effect on the animal population is disturbing and often unwittingly cruel. The effect on the human population isn't very healthy either. We aren't meant to sit on top of one another in rectangular cubicles peering out windows that don't open, breathing canned air and subjecting our minds to routine jolts of stress.

No one, even in 1944, could have foreseen the dramatic shift in our population. It's a sure bet horses didn't see it coming either.

Money burned a hole in Mother's pocket, as I mentioned earlier. She couldn't help but be seduced by a bright scarf, a shiny pair of earrings, or the thrill of a horse race. Oh, how she loved to bet on the horses: flat racing, steeplechasing, harness racing. Much of my childhood found me on the back side of the tracks. In those days, no one thought the sight of wagering would warp a young mind, so I could come and go as I pleased, for which I will forever be grateful. I can't understand why children are not allowed to attend racing but can be subjected to violence in the media around the clock. Perhaps we should rethink how we show the world to our children. Spending it with horses, for me anyway, was a wondrous experience. Mother, always decked out (she was a clotheshorse), would stroll along the shedrows point-ing out horses to me.

"Look at that cannon bone. Now, that's what I like to see."

The cannon bone is in the foreleg, between knee and hoof.

"Why?"

She squinted at me for a moment as the smoke from her ever-present Chesterfield drifted into her lovely gray eyes. "This horse is a chaser. When he jumps the brush or the timber, the bang first hits his hoof, and then the thin chain of bones above that, and then it will hit the cannon bone. A heavy cannon bone usually means a horse will last. A thin one"—she shook her head—"breaks like a twig." She made a gun out of her hand and fired, "Bang."

"Oh, Momma." I just hated the thought.

"Honey, you can't fix a broken leg in a good horse. They don't heal. They keep rebreaking the bone, and the poor beast suffers. You have to shoot them. It seems cruel, but it's a dreadful thing to let an animal suffer."

"Does a racehorse need a good cannon bone?"

"In truth, all horses do. That's why old Tweetie Byrd hunts Suzie Q. I wouldn't be caught dead in the hunt field on a draft. A lady should ride a Thoroughbred, and that's the end of it."

I loved all horses, even the paints and the Appaloosas with their beautiful coat patterns, but they were beyond the pale then in the hunt field. You wouldn't dare show up on a horse of color. Thankfully those days are gone and many more horses have the opportunity to foxhunt.

In some ways, foxhunting mirrors a horse's natural order. They're running in a herd, except for the staff horses, which are out alone. They're outside in a big space, not circling some track or show ring and putting stress on that inside shoulder. Horses can smell the fox better than we can, although not as handily as the hounds. And they are loved. Most foxhunters lavish care upon their horses. For one thing, you're together sometimes for four hours—even five, on those rare days when you rouse one fox after another—in sleet, in rain, in snow, in sunshine. The bond that's formed is deep.

Back on that shedrow I already understood that bond just by being around all the horses and meeting the special people who worked with them so closely. Mother loved a horse show and she was as happy to watch good Saddlebreds or a bracing steeplechase with perfectly conditioned Thoroughbreds. Naturally, she swanned about in something stunning so she became part of the show. I sometimes think one of the reasons she took me was because she could rest her drink on my head. She stood only five foot two, but as a child, I was still much shorter. This pleased her.

Our family was spread over Maryland, Virginia, and southern Pennsylvania. Mother's uncle, my Great-uncle Johnny Huff, owned a large stable between Baltimore and Green Spring Valley Hunt. He lost it when he was arrested for making book. But Mother got along with the new owner—well, not so new because Great-uncle Johnny went to prison way back in the Great Depression. Occasionally we'd drive out so I could play with a suitably calm animal, although I could get along with high-strung horses, too, and Mother eventually noticed this. I'm a whiz with a horse in that I can sometimes calm down a horse that someone else has jazzed up or who is naturally a little spiked. I have no idea why.

Confession time: as I have aged I am not as thrilled to be calming down hot horses or green ones. The jigging just wears me out. Gone is that youthful ego that shouts "I can do it." Now my motto is "I can do it, but that's what children are for." This is not to say I'm a good rider. What I am is tough.

Mother appreciated my devotion to hounds and dogs, but her special love was for horses and cats. When she saw I could talk to them, in a manner of speaking, she realized I could be very useful. She'd send me back to the shedrows on research missions. Whoever was running that day I was to check on and report. What was the condition of the coat? This was very important to her. Could I see their hooves? Was any horse improperly shod or past due? What was the animal's attitude? This mattered most of all to her, and it does to me, too.

I'd stroll along, peer into stalls, jabber with the grooms, who were goldmines of information, and not just about horses. Many of the grooms were Negro. We'd never say "black." That would have been rude. The word was "Negro," and if someone was highly respected, it was "colored gentleman."

Racing season, summer, meant stretches of sitting in a chair leaning against the side of a barn that was under the overhang to be in the shade. Work started before sunup, so by twelve you could take a long break unless your horse was running. No one wanted to leave the track. The excitement overpowered you. And the truth is, most of those grooms loved their horses. How it must have hurt when one was claimed or bought out from under the caretaker. For many owners, then and now, it's about money. For the grooms and for me, it's about the horses.

Those men were good to me. Maybe they got a kick out of a kid asking such pointed questions. Chances are they just liked kids.

If I asked "When did that horse bow?" the groom, if he didn't know me, was surprised.

A bow is a strain of the superficial flexor tendon, which is on the back of the foreleg above the fetlock (which is right above the hoof). It literally bows out in a convex manner. A long rest often takes care of it.

What I relayed to Mother factored into her bets. She was all business at the track, although most people wouldn't pick that up since she was a highly skilled, convivial flirt.

Foxhunting was different. No bets. She wasn't as enthusiastic, although she'd see everyone off. But of all the horse sports, this one was magic to me. Everything I loved was encompassed by this activity: foxhounds, horses, foxes, and the outdoors, to say nothing of the clothing. Just smashing.

Foxhunting is a fall and winter sport, so I'd stand there in my cowboy boots, or rubbers if it drizzled, protected by my sweater and a coat, absorbing everything.

Many of Mother's friends still walked the earth then. In their sixties, seventies, eighties, and a few in their nineties, they seized the day. Carpe diem. Unless crippled by pain or disease, no one enjoys life as much as someone who's lived a long time. It felt like the wealth of equine information was slipping away whenever one of these cronies would be "called home," as we say.

I figured I'd better visit them, one by one. Some of them, like Humphrey Finney, a partner in Fasig Tipton, an auction house, were well-known. But Humphrey passed before I could have a long chat liberally spiced with his favorite libation. His son, John, a Dickens scholar and successful trainer, exuded much of his father's charm, combined with a keen mind. He died young, but I had the opportunity to talk to him many times. Mother couldn't wait to hear the results of our talks on bloodlines. (Shortened version: Go back to Domino, Commando, Peter Pan, and always, always Teddy.)

In some cases, the conditions in which the former trainers and jockeys lived—most in Maryland, a few in Delaware, and more in Virginia—shocked me. No fund existed for older shedrow people (for lack of a better term). These people gave their lives to racing. Granted, when young, many of them blew their money on wine, women, and song, to say nothing of laying down bets at the window. But they did their jobs. By the time they realized the years were telling on them, they had families to support. Horse racing was all they knew. Most of them lacked the training to set up a business, even a simple one like repairing tack. A few were illiterate. Some found places in the good hunter/jumper barns or among foxhunters, but the track is an encompassing world: drama, danger, sexual escapades, and sometimes death to horse and human. Few wish to leave under their own steam. So they hung around until they could barely move.

One fellow—Angelfood was his nickname, the point being that angel food is white and Angel was black as the ace of spades—roared with good humor. What a fabulous attitude he had, sitting in his tiny apartment. But it was decent and at the edge of a big farm where he could do odds and ends.

These men, all men then, did not want to be idle. As happy as Mother was that Angel could get along (the farm being very close to Hanover Horse Farms, the nirvana of standardbreds) she was upset to hear of those who were barely getting by in little better than shacks with a wood-burning stove. I heat with one, but I have electric heat, too. These guys depended on wood to keep warm, and many cooked with it.

I bring up their condition because any one of these men would have been willing to endure more hardship if it had meant reuniting with some of the horses he loved.

This was back in the mid-seventies.

A few cried at the recollection of seeing good horses broken down and hauled off on the knacker's wagon. Some weren't broken down, just tuckered out. Boarding them at a pasture for a good rest would have brought most of them back. New careers could have been possible. But then, as now, flat racing is ruthless. No matter how they dress it up, it stinks. Horses are run too young, too hard. They break down and are cast off.

If those in flat racing wait for the government to clean up their act, so much the worse for them. It will produce results like the slaughter bill: more suffering than the suffering it was intended to relieve. Since horses can't be sold for meat value people let them starve . . . or worse, load them onto double-decker trucks to be hauled to Mexico. The conditions are horrible. The problem has been the treatment of horses awaiting slaughter. I'm not keen on slaughtering horses, but it's a quick death. Starvation is much worse. But here's the point: doing nothing will cost more money. Ultimately, the public may become so sick at watching horses break down that racing will be voted out.

That upsets me as much as the abuse I have seen, not just on the low-end tracks but at the high end, too. Are there good people in racing? Yes, some of the best. But for whatever reason, racing seems to have too many chiefs, and achieving cooperation takes the patience of all the giving saints. Plus, racing has lost some of its finest leaders in recent years. We just lost the incomparable racing journalist Joe Hirsch.

I stopped by to visit those old fellows. They spoke more eloquently than I can. I always brought treats and an envelope with cash, which I put in the bottom of the basket so they wouldn't have a fit in front of me. Why cash? Because no one with a grain of sense will send cash through the mail. I knew they wouldn't send the money back. And it wasn't a lot. I didn't have but so much, but I figured it would pay the rent for a month and buy groceries.

Now there are special funds for injured jockeys and their families. There are also organizations that help track workers with drinking and drug problems. Whether there are retirement plans or emergency funds for old trainers and grooms I don't know. I hope so.

Even more, I hope and pray that racing cleans up its act. When the 1986 Kentucky Derby winner, Ferdinand, a gentle, sweet horse, was sold to Japanese interests for stud and he faltered, they killed him. Ferdinand beat the 1987 Derby winner, Alysheba, in the Breeder's Cup Classic, too. Claiborne Farm in Paris, Kentucky, owned Ferdinand. His stud fee was thirty thousand dollars. His first crops didn't do well at the track. In 1994, they sold Ferdinand to Japan's JS Company. Placed on Hokkaido Island, he bred mares for six seasons. Business slowed. The owners either sold or gave him to Yoshikazu Watanabe, a horse dealer. JS never tried to reach Claiborne Farm or the Kech family, who originally bred Ferdinand. It was reported that he left the farm in Japan on February 3, 2001. He was sent to the killer.

The Hancocks of Claiborne Farm were sick, just sick. These are wonderful horse people. The Kech family was also horrified. They weren't the only ones. When the story broke in the United States we were all devastated. Kill a Kentucky Derby winner? Kill the 1987 Horse of the Year?

I pray there is a special hell for people who mistreat animals. The lowest chamber should have Yoshikazu Watanabe in it and the rest of those heartless money-grubbers.

There are enough death sentences here. Ferdinand was unbelievable. An average Thoroughbred is all the more likely to suffer when his career is over. It must be stopped.

A glorious show jumper called Sea King also landed on the knacker's truck. His former owner saw what was happening and did nothing. Too expensive to feed a horse past his prime. The owner never really recovered from his betrayal of Sea King. His wife left him—well, maybe not just over that, but I'm sure it was a factor. A nice man, he had suffered a big lapse of judgment, and Sea King paid for it.

You and I have a contract with animals. No court will honor it or even recognize it, just as no court will allow a child to press charges. As for animals, they can't argue for themselves. Bob Barker has just given one million dollars to the University of Virginia Law School for people to study animal law. God bless that man.

Every animal in the United States depends on the human being who owns it to honor his or her obligations. When the role of the animal is to generate cash, this contract falls apart as soon as the animal is no longer ringing up the cash register. Dog and cat owners also dump their pets, but for a large animal like a horse the problem is far greater.

Few people these days understand how to care for a horse or cow. Few people understand the animal's mind. These are prey animals.

Many people do understand that a horse is not a pet; it is a team member. What that means is that you work with your horse differently than you work with your cats and dogs. (The exception, of course, is the people who work with gun dogs and hounds.) A horse has a job to do. More to the point, if treated decently, the animal wants to work. Horses, like people, get bored. Idle hands do the Devil's work. Idle hooves can do the Devil's work, too. Usually their pranks are funny. Sometimes, like when a mare, in a mood, takes out part of your fence line, it's not. One night, just after sundown, three horses under my care got out of their large pasture. A tree weakened by a recent ice storm had fallen on the fence, and those bad boys got out and trashed my barn. I had to laugh once I finished cursing.

It all boils down to money.

The Thoroughbred Retirement Fund can do only so much. There are some other rescue leagues out there as well. I happen to know the Fund the best, as I have one of their former racehorses. I also take horses off the track before the Fund ever sees them. That's one less animal for them to house and feed. If I take them they must be able to foxhunt, so it depends on my being able to read the animal. So far I've done okay. I have five Thoroughbreds working at the moment, and one youngster coming along, too. He wasn't fast enough for the track but he's plenty fast enough for me.

One of Mother's distant relatives through marriage was Berta Jones, MFH of Farmington Hunt. Mrs. Jones had three former Kentucky Derby winners at her farm, Ingleside: Meridian, who won in 1911; Omar Khayyam, 1917; and Paul Jones, 1920. She hunted them. I hasten to add that Berta could ride—sidesaddle, no less. This was all before my time, but Mother always said that Berta showed us the way.

One other huge problem for anyone with stock is that Congress is made up of suburbanites and city boys—still mostly city boys. Every time taxes get raised, animals suffer. People only have but so much money, and targeting racing because there are some wealthy people in it is wrong. Who do you think provides jobs? A poor person? Hell, no. A rich one. Give them a tax break for everyone they hire. Well, I give up. It's too tempting, I guess, to demonize the rich. I'd love to see everyone of substance take their money right out of the country. Even for three months. Oh, my, would Congress sing a different tune.

But again, it's the animals that suffer. Small example: twenty years ago, as a farmer, I could income average. I had seven years in which to make a profit. Now, thanks to those blistering idiots on the north side of the Potomac, I must do it in four. Well, for the last three years we've had droughts. Instead of three to four hay cuttings per year I've harvested two, and the second one isn't worth much. I have to buy hay from the Midwest to feed the stock. Do my taxes reflect Mother Nature's bad hair years? Nope. Unless a region is labeled a disaster area there is no recognition of what bad weather can do to a farmer's profits. When the pine beetle destroyed half my timber crop there was no adjustment to taxes and no help from the government, either. And you wonder why the family farms are shrinking, and why animals are being abandoned? It isn't right, but when it comes down to a person feeding the kids or the cattle, the cattle are going to get cut loose if they can't be sold. It's horrifying to those of us who see it.

Sea King's dreadful end and his owner's sobs haunt me. Ferdinand's fate still brings tears to my eyes. If nothing else, no matter how wrongheaded I can be (me?), no matter how stupid (I admit it), I honor my commitments. I have made more promises to animals than to people, and your word is your honor, your life, your self-worth. You cannot break your word. You shouldn't break your word in Indiana, but you sure don't break it south of the Mason-Dixon Line. You bring shame on yourself and your whole family.

I've given my word to a rescued horse named Gunsmoke, and the other rescues that I acquired directly. I've given it to every hound, horse, cat, and dog on my farm. Even my chickens. I've given my word to my foxes, too.

If you've given yours, live up to it. Times are tough and going to get tougher. What do you give up? Hopefully not your house, but if you must, then you are obliged to find good homes for animals you can't feed.

People think I'm rich. I'm not on food stamps, but I'm in a profession that depends on the goodwill of the public. Chicken one day and feathers the next. One day people may no longer wish to read what I write. I'll be old news, washed up. As this is a country that worships the new and the young, I'm surprised it hasn't already happened. The last thing I represent is the new.

What's kept me in oats is my love of animals. It infuses everything I write, whether it's the mysteries or my stand-alone books. I finally figured out that millions of Americans truly love animals. Maybe they don't understand horses but they are willing to consider a prey animal's view of life. They may not be able to take on a horse but they'll send twenty dollars to the Thoroughbred Retirement Fund or swing by the SPCA and drop off a bag of cat food or dog kibble. I finally came to realize how many of my countrymen and women loved animals. A lot of them read me, so I can rescue larger animals than they can. The reason I work— and, yes, I do love writing, but the *real* reason I work—is for animals. People respond to that.

Since you love animals (or you wouldn't be reading this sentence), make a vow with me: no more Sea Kings. No more Ferdinands. Let's do what we can. I know you honor your contract with animals. Now you and I must honor those that have been broken. One by one, we can save animals. If we join forces, think how much more we can do.

Parrots are smart, feisty birds, and some of them are real chatterboxes. I was
never on good terms with my paternal grandmother but her parrot, Franklin,
was a great pal. One summer, I taught him to say unchristian words . . .
a parting gift for Grandmother Carrie when we moved away to Florida.
Photo courtesy of John Garcia.

When I was ten, Mother and Dad took me on a trip to Fort Lauderdale, Florida. It was very different from the world I knew.

The Atlantic Ocean was fascinating. One morning at sunrise, we walked along the flat beaches with semicoarse sand. Catapulting out of the water were sleek dolphins. Transfixed, all we could do was stare at their beauty and their obvious enjoyment of life. The dolphins put on quite a show, and then as they passed, a devil ray floated silently in their wake, like a great black ghost breaking above the surface of a calm sea. Its fins turned upward and inward, the great fish glided along while the water rolled over it like an ascending cascade. The first rays of light caught the water and tiny rainbows streamed off those black fins.

Did Peter the Great, who dreamed up the stupendous fountains at Peterhof in Russia, ever see a devil ray? Is that where Rastrelli, whom he hired to design them, got his ideas? Probably not, but if he had, he would have been as overcome as we were.

Schools of little fish came close to the shore, thousands of silver coins darting and dashing under clear water as the sun turned everything from blood to red to scarlet, then pink and finally gold, so much gold.

My parents fell in love with this small, quiet city of thirty thousand people that was laced with canals. And the following year, 1955, they announced that we were moving there.

While I appreciated the beauty of the subtropics, all I wanted was hounds, horses, and farming. Dad inquired about foxhunting clubs. None. I couldn't believe it. I'd learned by the age of five that pitching a hissy wasn't going to get me anywhere. It produced the opposite effect. I tried to get used to the idea, and hoped for the best.

The Browns ran a grocery and meat market in West York, and by 1955 our family had been in business since before the Revolutionary War. I don't know the location of the original store, but the West York location was excellent. Dad sold his share to his two brothers. The town went into shock. No one really believed we would leave. Aunt Mimi was one step ahead of a running fit.

Dad's parents, Carrie and Reuben Brown, practically had a grand mal seizure although they were more emotionally reserved than Mother's family and therefore rarely capable of producing much excitement.

Grandma and Grandpa Brown were stunningly good-looking people. She was flat-out beautiful even after four children (one died young) and subsequent weight gain. She was never fat but she was broad. He looked as he did in his wedding pictures, but by the time I knew him his hair had turned steel gray. With age he stooped. They were town people but understood the country because Reuben bought cattle and horses for himself. He could judge the meat-to-bone ratio and had a good idea of fat content, too. He passed this on to Dad, and Dad took me out with him when he went to buy cattle. I learned a little. I learned far more about horses, but I liked the cattle and hoped that once we were in Florida, Dad would be buying Brahmans so I could learn about them.

In the days before our departure, we visited Dad's family just about every day. This was no picnic for me.

The thing about the Browns was that they didn't like me. I wasn't their blood, plus I was illegitimate to boot. Julia Brown's mother, Big Mimi, was my natural mother's mother. So Sadie Huff's sister was Big Mimi's. Sadie's daughter, eighteen, became pregnant without benefit of marriage. The result, me. Carrie Brown couldn't believe her adored son would adopt me.

How many times did I hear that I could not ever belong to the United Daughters of the Confederacy, the Daughters of the American Revolution, or the Colonial Dames? My yet-to-be-produced oldest son could never be a member of the Society of Cincinnatus. I hated it. I especially loathed Carrie Brown. She only spoke to me to give me an order. "Dinner is ready, come to the table." She never asked me what I liked. And as I have told you earlier, I was raised to speak only when spoken to. But she allowed me to read *National Geographic,* so when I was sentenced to the purgatory of her house (a pretty one) I sat by the great bay window and read this excellent magazine from cover to cover. Still do.

Reuben, hardly a barrel of fun, was kinder. He smiled when he saw me. He offered me his hand, as a gentleman does to a lady in our part of the world. He always wore a three-piece suit, his thick gold chain draped across his vest, a gold watch tucked into his vest pocket. Whenever he came back from the store, he kissed Carrie, for theirs was a good marriage. He'd remove his coat, she'd hang it, brush it, then return to her chores. He'd roll up his shirtsleeves but wouldn't remove his vest or his tie. If the day had been wearing he might sip a bit of scotch or bourbon. I never saw the bottle, for the liquid was in a crystal decanter. In the summer, Carrie brought him some untea (we call unsweetened tea "untea"), and in the winter, a cup of coffee. He'd go to his chair, pull the chain on the beautiful Tiffany lamp, and read the paper. I read the magazine. We remained in silence together but compatible.

The funny thing was that the house was not quiet, because Mamaw (Carrie) owned a big green parrot who felt compelled to comment on all and sundry. If Mother wore a red blouse he'd yell "Red." If Aunt Mimi's dog trotted into the kitchen on a visit, he'd call the dog's name, to Butch's great annoyance. The bird missed nothing.

Carrie's large kitchen was flooded with sunlight. For years they had a wood-burning stove, but by the time I came into the world, Reuben had bought her a fancy porcelain model. She rose at four o'clock and baked bread, every single morning. The aroma of that house on Diamond Street lifted you up the minute you crossed the threshold. Famed for her cooking skills and her baking, Carrie was also sought after for advice. She, like Mother, was a power in her church, and like Mother, her gardening skills were impressive. Her kitchen was her kingdom! Spotless, there was a place for everything and everything in its place. What that woman could do with ingredients, everything fresh, nothing packaged, would make today's high-priced chefs blush.

She'd hum away as she prepared her next triumph while

Franklin called out "Hello," "Don't forget the salt," and a variety of things that made you laugh.

Before I was born, Carrie had a female parrot named Polly, a wedding present from her husband. Polly lived well into her forties. When she went to the Great Parrot in the Sky, Reuben gave Carrie another parrot. Franklin was named for Ben Franklin because he cost one hundred dollars (a fortune then). Reuben was not a man to throw away his money. He wasn't cheap, but he was watchful. He dearly loved his wife, and when Polly passed, Carrie had what we used to call a sinking spell. He found the most beautiful parrot he could, and sure enough, my grandmother bounced right back.

One time, from all the way at the other end of the house, I heard "Roses, roses, roses," followed by "Japanese beetles." I put down the *National Geographic* and walked outside on that mild June day to check the rosebushes under Franklin's big window. Sure enough: Japanese beetles on the cadmium yellow roses.

Franklin showed me that birds are smart. Some types may be smarter than others, but if you've ever visited with parrots, mynahs, or macaws or watched any of the blackbird family, they solve problems, observe intently, and gossip indiscriminately.

Filled with excitement, I strolled into the garden. Mighty rose blossoms in every shade massed along the picket fence shouted "Summer!" Who taught Franklin to say "Japanese beetles"? Maybe he overheard it, because he caught on fast. Mamaw would not abide swearing. She didn't even tolerate "darn," although you could say "fudge." Well, *she* could say it. I couldn't. But no swearing in front of Franklin because he'd remember and repeat it later.

A plan hatched in my mind. Mom and Dad planned to leave town shortly. School was out. They'd already sold our wonderful place looking over the valley. Everything was packed except for a few clothes and kitchen items. The moving van would pull up in ten days. No one could organize like Julia Buckingham Brown.

I still miss Mother tremendously, and Dad, too. What would I give to have Mother run my daily life and to have Dad in the kennel with me? Every woman needs a husband and a wife. Don't think I'll get too far with that, but since we have dispensed with the serving class, thanks to outrageous income taxes, payroll taxes, capital gains taxes, and minimum wages, etc., every person is on overload trying to do it all themselves.

The next time I was at my grandparents' house before we moved, I ran to Franklin, who looked at me and said "Treats." I gave him a bit of cuttlebone, which he daintily grasped with one claw while keeping a firm hold on one of his many perches with the other. He liked to swing around from perch to perch, which made me laugh.

Mamaw paid no attention to me. I whispered, "Shit."

From that day forth, until we left for Florida, each time I visited my father's parents I made certain to whisper (or say out loud if no one was around) "Shit."

Meanwhile Mother found a home for my beloved collie, Ginger, who I trained after Chaps passed away. She was a tricolor with that eagerness to please that the herding dogs have. Charlie and Cappy went to Uncle Jim, Dad's uncle, as he enjoyed hunting a brace. Mother said it would be wrong to take Ginger to Florida because of her heavy coat. I protested, but orders were orders. I was expected to acclimate, but Ginger was not.

In retrospect, she was right, for houses didn't have air-conditioning then. Thick hair is a burden for a dog in the semi-tropics even with air-conditioning. Apart from the heat they get fungi and other conditions. Ginger went to a farm where she had a great life, herding cattle. I missed her the minute I handed over her leash.

Tuffy went to Aunt Gertrude, a rotund woman but beautiful. She'd been married to Mom's brother, Bucky, movie-star handsome and bursting with devilment. He died in his thirties. Gertrude never found another man as handsome or full of fun as Bucky. Again, Mother said Tuffy would suffer in the heat. Yes, I could have a cat and a dog, but they had to be born in Florida. She also informed me that it would take us a year to acclimate. She was right about that, too.

We visited PopPop's grave, leaving flowers. I left dog biscuits. Just seemed like the thing to do. I vowed to my departed port-in-a-storm that the day would come when I would hunt my own pack. I promised I would do him proud. I'm still trying.

The van came. We climbed into the Chrysler (a terrific car back then) with enough clothes to get us to Florida. No tears, but I was wretched. Well, if life hands you a lemon, make lemonade. I was determined to make the best of it.

In our new hometown, there were countless new wonders to appreciate. Flocks of wild parrots flying in an azure sky look like large pieces of confetti twirling about. Parrot feathers, built for speed unlike owl feathers built for silence, allow these chatterboxes and outright screechers to dip, dive, soar, and turn one-eighties. Because of their feather construction, when they swoop low you can hear the rustle. If the flock is large it's really something to hear that sound.

Dad took me to farms in Davie, the pastures filled with a

broad, flat-bladed grass that would have been weeded out in the Mid-Atlantic. There I saw my first herd of Brahman cattle, a large white breed with a distinctive hump. They are not famous for their good personalities. Dad kept me from wiggling under the barbed wire fence to pet them. Since the 1950s I'm pretty sure responsible breeders have improved temperament, just as they have improved temperament in Angus. Unfortunately they've shortened the legs in Angus in an effort to increase the muscle-to-bone ratio, and this author thinks it's a dreadful disservice to the animal.

No herds of my favorite, horned Herefords, or even polled Herefords. Florida was all Brahmans.

But I liked the parrots, the hibiscus, the ixona, the restorative salt breezes. The coconut palms, the queen palms, and the royal palms lent a stately air to the flatlands. I'm not a flatlander, but if it's dressed up a little I can withstand the monotony.

Although I did find things to like, no foxhunting was a dagger to the heart. Did anyone have hounds? Dad found some gentleman who hunted beagles, and of course there are always coonhounds in the South. But I was not yet eleven, and grown men with tobacco in their cheeks don't really want someone else's kid tagging along, especially a girl.

We drove through the center of the state, the citrus groves unrolling for miles. That I liked, for I wanted to farm. But Mom and Dad had turned fifty and had no intention of farming. Their dream was to live in the suburbs. Children are hostages to their parents. I lived in that pink house until I turned seventeen and graduated from high school. Off I went, never to return, except for Mother's birthdays, March 6.

• • •

A few weeks after we had settled into our new home, flamingo pink, Gertrude sent us a photo of Tuffy. Tuffy was already as fat as Gertrude.

The other surprising thing was that Dad received a letter in his mother's elegant handwriting that contained shocking, shocking news. Franklin had said "Shit." Apparently quite often.

Tuxedo and Sneaky Pie were great friends, napping together and sharing a food bowl. When Tuxedo first wandered onto my farm, he was three months old, rail thin, and covered in mites. Now he's old, fat, and happy, and he and his owner, my friend Betsy Sinsel who adopted him, truly love each other. *Photo by Betsy Sinsel.*

Learning to Adapt

Living in Fort Lauderdale, Florida, in the mid-1950s, I was surrounded by an exotic natural world that was completely different from the Piedmont I loved so much. Florida was a surreal place where it might be pouring rain on one side of the street with brilliant sunshine on the other. The subtropics challenge those of us raised in the higher latitudes. I had much to learn from this exotic new environment.

In South Florida, night-blooming jasmine infused the air, brushed my skin, promised magic. The smells and sounds are sui generis, unique to this patch of subtropics. Much of what you see delights.

Other things can kill you. Dig down, hit a pocket of mango gas, that's the last breath you'll take. Fool around on the jetties jutting out into the ocean without paying attention to where the schools of little fish are, and a shark might consider you lunch, or a barracuda might be tempted to see how sweet human meat is. Smaller creatures come armed. Mosquitoes bite like the devil, as do sand flies, and then there are palmetto bugs and cockroaches large enough to pay rent.

On the bright side, I can remember a flock of flamingos escaping the infield of Gulfstream Park racetrack, filling the sky with a brilliant pink cloud. They returned shortly after this soaring moment because life was good at Gulfstream once upon a time.

Across the Florida East Coast railroad tracks reposed a relatively large swamp. Fort Lauderdale was still small then. As I mentioned earlier, a city of thirty thousand people was a kind of paradise. It wasn't my paradise but it was seductive. I often miss it, especially when the poinciana trees bloom in March. All over Fort Lauderdale the eye is caught by huge orange canopies filled with birds singing away.

The swamp lacked such attractions, but it did have alligators. Now the whole thing has been drained. The alligators have all been shot (a sin) and houses sit on landfill. They'll eventually tilt and crack, if they haven't already.

Alligators scared me but I had to watch them. They'd lie on the banks sunning themselves, lazy creatures. Something would attract them and they'd slither into the swamp. When they opened their mouths it was impressive. Many a dog has made the mistake of getting too close to those open mouths only to discover how quickly an alligator can move. I never tested it.

Garfish, at a quick glance, can resemble sleek, small alligators. They're actually a kind of needlefish with sharp, nasty teeth, and they can be aggressive. They'll swim in close to the shore. I kept my distance from those as well.

Starting in the seventh grade, I endured two years of schooling at the Naval Air Station. The famous Lost Squadron took off from

Naval Air long before I attended school there. By ninth grade, Sunrise Junior High was completed. I could walk to school, whereas Naval Air was over ten miles away. There was no air-conditioning. I didn't have air-conditioning until I was in my forties. But you don't miss what you don't know, so it felt completely natural to sit in those two-tiered wooden barracks sweating as our teachers droned on. A few were good, but most of them had tired of teaching young people long ago. And none of them ever displayed the slightest interest in our natural environment.

Surrounded by the natural odor of sulphur gas from some of the waters, sweet-smelling flowers, heavy salt scent from the sea, I had no one to teach me. I can't say I loved the environment as I loved and continue to love the Mid-Atlantic, but I was fascinated.

My salvation was the local library, a small building downtown on Middle River that I believe had once been a house. It felt like a house, anyway. Mom or Dad would drop me off, or sometimes I'd walk. It was four miles away. Other times I'd take the bus. Once I was there, I read and read.

I also went out and observed the natural world firsthand, and I can still vividly recall what I found.

Swamp foxes darted about, along with many forms of wild felines, including what we called the Florida panther, a sleek, fast-moving creature that could startle you. Sand sharks swam around the canals using their tails in a manner that fascinated me. Most big fish have powerful tails, but the sand shark's seemed extra flexible. Like their bigger brethren in the ocean, they look fearsome. Among these ocean sharks, the hammerheads stood out, never failing to startle with those strange eyes. The sand sharks left us alone, though. I never tested the ocean sharks by being in the water with them.

The creature that fascinated me most was the manatee. "Manatee" first came into the English language in 1554 according to my *Oxford English Dictionary*. An aquatic marine animal, this wonderful creature is sometimes called a sea cow.

I observed my first manatee on a little bridge that stretched from Fort Lauderdale into Wilton Manor on Northeast Fifteenth Street. A little curve in the water there allowed all manner of aquatic creatures to fiddle and faddle.

Manatees are large, brown, and oddly shaped, kind of like a flattened beanbag. They eat plants—no flesh—and they like shallow waters. They can dive, though, and they can move with fair speed, given their shape and size. They weigh around a thousand pounds and they have a few natural predators including sharks and alligators. But frankly, people are their main problem. Manatees can get cut up by outboard propellers. Someone not a Floridian or a person interested in nature would see one and scream bloody murder. Fortunately few of these folks owned guns or harpoons. Occasionally the police would receive a call about manatees. I often wonder what they said to the panicked soul on the other end of the line. Eighty percent of police calls are nuisance calls, I would imagine, and twenty percent must be horrible things.

Anyway, my fascination grew. I'd ride up Fifteenth Street on my trusty blue Schwinn with the balloon tires, go down the embankment, and sit by the canal, wondering if I'd see one of my beanbags. Often I did. Once one came close to enough give me the once-over. I guess I didn't pass muster, because he turned around and left me flat.

The manatee's maneuverability impressed me. One of my classmates reminded me of this aquatic mammal. He didn't look like a brown beanbag but he resembled a block. No shape. However, he was fast and played left tackle. Left tackles are smart. He played through high school and college, and when he came back home he started a turf business. Underline "successful" three times.

As long as we protect manatees they'll be successful, too.

Sea turtles astonished me. Once a year the females would clamber up from the Atlantic, dig, and lay their eggs. They'd twirl around on their bellies once they'd pulled sand back over their future offspring. Then they'd slowly amble back to the ocean. They were huge. And I marveled at the fact that I was looking at animals who were probably seventy or eighty years old. I don't know if they can breed at those ages, but you'd see the turtles who didn't come onto shore waiting in the shallows for their companions.

Age impresses me in any creature. Part of it is luck, but it also means that animal is wise. We place so much emphasis on book smarts that we miss emotional wisdom, wisdom about the self, the ability to read the environment. Long-lived creatures have figured these things out. Many scientists will tell you an animal has no sense of self, of its own individuality. Bunk. And prudence isn't fear. There are prudent animals.

The A-plus students, the Oxford scholars, often lead lives that are emotional disasters, but the kid who somehow has the sense not to drink and drive, marries the right person, finds work that keeps the heart full, that prudent kid keeps going and going. He or she may never be lauded for excellence in their field but will be well-rounded and successful in life.

Of course, some academics and left-brain folks get it. Survival, I mean. But this sinks in later in life. The convention is that stupid people cause trouble. Some do. They usually wind up dead or in jail. I think more trouble is caused by people who may be experts in one field but are dolts about life in general.

Animals don't suffer these problems. The dumb ones are killed off early. They don't get to pass on those dumb genes. The unlucky ones perish early, too.

Due to air travel, diseases that affect animals can be carried to our country literally on people's pants legs. That, too, kills people and animals. Witness the West Nile virus.

Our future well-being and that of other creatures now depends on the human ability to correctly assess a threat and react swiftly. Remember the dreadful slaughter of cattle in England as a result of hoof-and-mouth disease? Someone dawdled. That's all it took. The cost in lives, livelihoods, and grief can never truly be calculated.

The human animal must now "be sober, be vigilant," as Muriel Spark once put it. When you factor in cultural differences it seems inevitable that in the future, thousands if not millions of certain animals (chickens, for instance) will die, and millions of us may die with them.

Florida couldn't prepare me for this. Nothing could. But Florida and its creatures taught me adaptability to new weather conditions. They also taught me that beauty is only skin deep. Thank you, Miss Manatee.

Godzilla is a character. She rides this ATV daily. She'll sit in it for hours, waiting for a driver to show up. Her philosophy is simple: What's yours is mine and what's mine is mine. She belongs in Congress. *Photo by Judy Pastore.*

Don't Judge a Dog by Its Appearance

Once we moved into the "pink palace" in Florida, Mother made good on her promise of a cat and a dog. As it turned out, the dog was never to be mine, but the cat was.

We visited the SPCA. I'd never been to one. The visit upset me, all those sad eyes, all those abandoned animals. Mother swore she'd never take me back, but I did adopt a white kitten with a few black spots and named her Skippy.

The dog, however, had to be well bred. Where did Mom get this bee in her bonnet? I wanted a foxhound. Forget that. Her comeback was that at seventy pounds, a foxhound is too big. Not as a big as a Great Dane, I'd reply to no avail. She read up on the different breeds and found a breeder of miniature poodles. The word "miniature" is misleading because they are the size of a Schnauzer (a fabulous dog). Dad traded in the Chrysler for a Plymouth whose tail fins made me think of the fish I'd been watching so closely. Mother borrowed the car, driving along at her usual blistering pace. The breeder in the northwest section of town kept a tidy place. Mother picked out a black male puppy without consulting me. Well, that was okay. Mom had an eye for conformation with dogs, but I actually think that even then, mine was better. She did pick the best pup in the litter, handed over a lot of money (a couple of good days at the track). Home we drove with the puppy in my lap.

Sunshine turned into the light of Mom's life. The training fell to me. At first I was mortified to be seen with a poodle. Thank God she never gave the dog a show cut. I would have put a paper bag over my head. Then I read about poodles, discovering that they were hunting dogs. Maybe he wouldn't be but so bad.

Smart, clean, eager to please, and what an easy fellow to work with. I did like him, but he was clearly Mother's dog. He liked me, too, but dogs are like people. There is special chemistry, and those two loved each other. He'd escort her on all her walks. He'd shoot into the car to ride shotgun. She couldn't take him to the tracks, as dogs were forbidden. He didn't attend church services. But other than that, they were inseparable.

Her lifelong love affair with poodles began with Sunshine. She bought herself dresses with poodles on them, poodle purses, poodle costume jewelry. At least she didn't buy glasses with poodle appliqués.

By now Aunt Mimi and her family had also turned their backs on the ancestral breeding grounds to move to Florida. The two sisters couldn't function without each other. Butch, the legendary Boston Bull, had passed away. Aunt Mimi, needing to be different, wouldn't have a poodle. Instead, she bought a Pekinese.

Dear God, now everything was Chinese. Chin, the indulged Pekinese, inspired my aunt to shop for clothing and jewelry in the same way that Sunshine inspired Mother. Our fear was Aunt Mimi would go all the way and we'd sit down to supper at her house only to be handed chopsticks.

The effect these dogs had on the ever-competing sisters was not lost on their husbands. Uncle Merle and Dad learned before I came into this world that if you make a woman happy, she makes you happy. Uncle Merle found Aunt Mimi a gorgeous Chinese silk dress, the kind with a high collar. As her figure was lovely, before we knew it, Aunt Mimi's wardrobe rivaled Mrs. Chiang Kai-shek's.

Mother fumed. One could find only so many poodle dresses and sweaters. She had a small black poodle painted on the driver's door of the car, embellished with her initials, J.E.B., underneath. Her straw hat, a real Montecristo, was set off by a red hatband with black poodles embroidered thereon.

I was finding out that animals can affect people in ways I never considered. And I sure learned the value of keeping a woman happy. Pay attention to her and do what she says. How exhausting that seemed to me. But back then I didn't fathom the payoff. That occurred to me later. How smart Dad and Uncle Merle were! And how spoiled were Chin and Sunshine, along with Aunt Mimi and Mother.

Mother always said, "If you love someone you've got to spoil them a little."

This quip usually was pronounced when I was performing a hateful chore like washing the jalousie windows.

"When do I get spoiled?"

She'd take a drag. "When you find the right man. I'm not going to spoil you. Bad for your moral fiber."

Florida was turning into a different kind of education. I also learned to eat egg rolls and wonton soup and never, never to criticize the beloved Chin or Sunshine.

While awash in Mother's poodle paraphernalia at home, Sunshine taught me that preferences are preferences and not to judge a book by its cover. He was a real dog and he could hunt.

When we moved to Florida, I missed the horses terribly. But thanks to the kindness of one of my classmates, a girl who was a member of the Juniorettes, I was invited to spend time with her family's Quarter horses. Now I have Quarter horses of my own. *Photo by Judy Pastore.*

Humans Learn to Compromise

I spent my formative years in Florida trying to figure out the dividing line between animals and humans—what made us different or special, how we ended up in charge.

I still don't know the answer, though most humans are convinced they are at the top of the food chain. Back then, I was learning over and over how each species had adapted to the environment, often swiftly. Humans seemed to be much slower at this, although everything I read kept telling me how wonderfully adaptable humans are. I didn't find that to be the case. Most of the people I knew were like butterflies with a pin through them. They could flap their wings but they weren't flying. They were impaled on belief systems that bore no correspondence to reality, caught up in dead-end relationships, alcoholism, and the worst vice of all: self-righteousness.

On the other hand, I observed something about humans that alligators, sea turtles, flamingos, dogs, cats, horses didn't share. Humans could compromise. Compromise is only possible when both parties can recognize, in some small way, the validity of the other party's concerns and arguments. Animals never compromise, though they do submit.

While I was trying to understand the world in which I'd been dropped, I blasted into my teens. Wasn't so bad. Mostly it was marvelous fun, kind of like when your puppy turns six months old. From six months to two years in a dog's life corresponds to our teen years: falling over our own feet, bubbling with enthusiasm, sulking off, committing one blunder after another, cavorting like crazy with other puppies our own age.

Backtalk appears. So do regular slaps in the face, usually richly deserved. This, too, is like rapping your pup on the rear end when it tears up that new blouse you'd put on the chair. Poor Mom. She bore the brunt of it but she gave as good as she got, coming out on top.

One girl at school, a member of the Juniorettes (I was an Anchor Club member), lived in Davie and her family had Quarter horses. My experience had always been with Thoroughbreds and Percherons. Through her kindness in allowing me to visit her, I could study another type of equine. Kept me out of trouble.

Quarter horses are built a little like fullbacks in football, or maybe more like baseball catchers. Their hindquarters are round and quite powerful, and so are their chests. There's a joke among Thoroughbred people that Quarter horses have man boobs. Thoroughbreds, while they muscle up, present a more refined, elegant appearance. A Quarter horse can hunch down on his hindquarters to hold a roped calf or steer. They are handy, usually very kind and easy to work with. You might find one with a long stride and fluid gait, but here again they differ from the Thoroughbred, often moving in a choppier fashion. I learned to respect them.

Having no tack, I'd hop up bareback using a hackamore (no bridle) and off we'd go. Linda had her own Western tack. I had nothing. She was a cowgirl. Florida was filled with cowboys because of all the cattle. Florida these days is God's waiting room, but there are still some tough country people out there in sand spurs. I'd never seen barrel racing and couldn't believe how low the Quarter horse could get, spinning around a barrel. They defied gravity.

That and tennis kept me out of Mother's hair. She'd haul me to her horse-racing jaunts. At Hialeah and Gulfstream we'd cruise the shedrows. The more I did this the more I wanted to do it. Once into high school, a mix of great fun and a couple of heartbreaks, I thought about college. I wanted to work with animals.

Many young people who love animals want to become veterinarians. I didn't. I'm not called to medicine on any level, and you aren't going to be a good doctor unless you are called, just as a minister is called. What I wanted to do was breed Thoroughbreds and foxhounds. Obviously, I wasn't going to stay in Florida. The Thoroughbred industry in Florida was just taking off in Ocala but there were no foxhounds. Actually, before my time, there was a hunt club in Coral Gables, and now there are many, including one of the best in the United States, Live Oaks. These clubs face quite difficult conditions: weather, heat, rampant development. The masters and hounds have risen to the occasion.

I cautiously mentioned to Dad that I'd like to major in agriculture, specializing in animal husbandry. Dad knew how much I loved animals. He pretended not to know that Mother haunted the tracks but he knew I had an affinity for Thoroughbreds. He didn't discourage me, but he gave me platinum advice.

"Country ways are dying. You want to farm but you won't make any money unless you own at least a thousand acres and rent more. If you want to make money you'll wind up working for a large agricultural company. The big fish are eating up the small."

He didn't need to tell me about how the urbanization of America was reordering political power. In short: cities get what they want. Country people get screwed. The votes are in the cities and suburbs. Those people can't distinguish buckwheat seed from orchard grass seed, or a Walker hound from a coonhound. They know things I don't, and I respect that. I'm not sure it works in reverse.

One small example, minimum wage, reflects city business. In the county I can provide housing and transportation. I get no tax credit for this and I must pay a "city" wage. And hey, have you noticed the number of unemployed recently? There is a relationship. I can't hire the people I need. I can't afford it. So multiply my economic reality by thousands of farmers. What's wrong with a two-tiered system of wages: one for industry, one for agriculture?

Back to my career choice: Mother joined Dad. She didn't mock all the career ideas I'd bandied about since I was tiny. The most unrealistic of these was an idea I came up with when I was around ten. I wanted to be a movie star so I could support everyone and have a stable as big as my Uncle Johnny's. (He lost it before I was born because he made book. Now the state does it. It's called off-track betting.)

Mother said farming was hard work but she knew I was up to it. She had made sure of that by working my tail off. I'm eternally grateful. When your family sets high but realistic expectations they are doing you a favor. You learn to deliver the goods. You learn to be part of a team.

"Mom, all I want to do is farm and hunt."

Dad chimed in, "That's a good life, but honey, the only people who will be able to do that by the time you're out there will be those with inherited wealth."

"Or those who hit it big," Mother added. "Regular people aren't going to make it. Stinks."

Dad, in that deep voice I can still hear, said, "You have a gift with animals, too. God gave you two gifts."

This was new to me.

"Three. She can argue like a goddamned lawyer." Mother exhaled the longest blue plume of smoke.

Dad laughed. "You have imagination."

Just where this was going to take me I didn't know, but I did know I could write a little. My teachers had always praised me. I love praise. I read promiscuously. Language was like music to me. I could write in the Latinate style—much of eighteenth and nineteenth century literature is like that—but I could also pare it down to the bone. We can thank Gertrude Stein and her great imitator (far more accessible than Gerty) Hemingway for that.

Worth a try.

Skippy the cat and I walked everywhere together. He rode in the car, too. He read the library books I took home as I thought more and more about being an English major. Just how I was going to hook that up with horses, foxhounds, timber, and hay, I didn't know. But I was taught "Trust yourself, trust the Lord, and keep putting one foot before the other."

Dad died suddenly of a heart attack on July 13, 1961. Not only did Mother, Aunt Mimi, Uncle Merle, and I mourn, so did Sunshine, Skippy, and even that spoiled rotten Chin. So many people and animals loved my father.

With Dad gone I really couldn't be indulgent. I needed to help out. Aunt Mimi wanted me to go right to work. Mother knew I had one year of high school left and we figured I could work after school. She didn't discourage me from going to college. Nor did she encourage me to go.

A career in farming seemed hopeless. I kept thinking about animals. Each animal is born with a body and skills to survive in its environment. How could I use what I had: physical power and speed in a small package, the ability to read nature's signs quickly? Oh, not as quick as a fox, but very fast for a woman. The other gift, a fighting heart, was going to have to pull me through.

On to college I slogged. Did I enjoy myself? I made friends who are still my friends, but I lived apart from animals. That's hell for me.

I knew Skippy loved me, and Dad's love never died. His body left. The love remained.

I learned that love knows no boundaries. And I learned later on that I had been given good advice.

Hounds taught me to follow my heart, hence I am never lost.
Photo by Danielle A. Durkin.

Finding My Way

The core American emotion is loneliness. Our earliest litera-ture, which I would put at James Fenimore Cooper, pinpoints this. Melville also allows us to feel our smallness from a perch on a topsail. These two New Yorkers wrote about the wildness of our continent and the power of animals. That power is obvious in *Moby-Dick*. But Cooper, although focusing on the intersection between various Indian tribes, the British, and the colonists, pro-vides glimpses of how untamed the land was. In some parts of our country, it still is. If he wandered above Saratoga, Cooper would not feel out of place. The Atlantic Ocean remains eternal. Mel-ville would understand.

Anyone from those pre–Revolutionary years who hiked into the Appalachian chain today would be surprised at the trails and the Skyline Drive, but other than that, the hawks still stop over there on their way south in the fall, the bears do as they please, and the bobcats stare at you with large, gorgeous eyes.

Florida is shot, except for the Everglades, which must be pro-tected no matter what the price. The rim of the Gulf of Mexico, dubbed the Redneck Riviera, would shock early settlers.

The Dakotas, and much of Wyoming, might not depress our ancestors. Montana's eastern or plains side still looks much the same. The western side, thanks to its great beauty, has been gobbled up by mere millionaires now ousted by billionaires. However, they aren't putting up parking lots, so that's to the good.

The far reaches of the Pacific Northwest host the lumber industry, which causes dissension, but Oregon and Washington state maintain their wildness. California is gone, an incalculable loss to those of us who love nature. California, like Florida, hosts an environment unique. South Florida is semitropical, whereas southern California is semiarid. The loss of animal habitat, the killing of the animals themselves, can never be reversed.

Once humans kill off enough animals they turn to killing one another. So it seems to me. I can't change it, but I do want to escape it.

At age nineteen, however, I found myself at the heart of Murder Central. Now a junior at New York University, I lived in a hovel during the destructive years in New York. You couldn't walk through Central Park at night. You couldn't walk through any park at night. Drugs created much of the misery, although there had to be other reasons, too. When a city fails on so many levels, there's more than one cause. The whole nation seemed to be convulsing. It's just that one notices things first in New York. When I was little people didn't lock their doors in New York or any major city. Melville certainly wouldn't have left his post office job because people were, as the expression has it, "going postal." Colliding with this was the rise of serial killers covered in newspapers and on TV (I didn't have one, but I sure heard about it) as though they were movie stars. Surely this must have encouraged other imbalanced minds to seek fame.

Technologically advanced as we are, I don't think we are particularly civilized. We haven't lived together for enough centuries to be a civilization. A culture, yes. A civilization, no.

Berlin was founded in A.D. 1000, give or take. The Italians consider the Germans much less civilized than themselves. Imagine how we look to any European, to say nothing of someone from an ancient Asian country.

The only animals I saw in New York City were squirrels, pigeons, house dogs. How I wound up in these city barrens was a tribute to ambition and scholarship. Apart from the lack of animals, the vulgarity of the place often upset me. People spoke harshly, sometimes obscenely. I was a long way from Dixie.

Mother struggled after Dad died. I worked odd jobs and sent home twenty dollars a month. I always sent catnip, too. Latin took some study. Greek took a lot and I wasn't very good at it. Working and studying proved difficult. I learned that in order to advance I would have to surrender a social life. That was okay. It was worth it.

Then I fell in love and everything changed. A tiny six-week-old gray tabby with extra toes was being carried into the cat shelter on Greenwich Avenue (read: death sentence). I plucked her out of the carton before the two little girls passed through the door. The two girls forced to give up the kittens cried and cried. I could only take one. I wished I could have taken them all, but I saved one. And she saved me.

There was just enough jingle in my pocket for cat food and some eggs. I put the little girl in my jacket pocket as I bought the food and raced back to West Fifteenth Street, where I lived in a cold-water flat on the fifth floor. I had no bed, slept on blankets on the floor. I did my schoolwork on some wooden crates I'd hauled up from the street along with a chair from which the stuffing protruded. I named my new kitten Baby Jesus.

She ate. She purred. She crawled into the blankets with me. I hid her in my Greek cloth bag. She attended classes, sleeping in the bag. As she grew she was harder to hide but more self-sufficient. I could leave her in the apartment, although whenever I could, I took her along. She completed a class in Latin. Livy. Livy is as elegant as Tacitus is not, and both were difficult to translate. You can either be grammatically accurate or stylish. It's hard to be both. I wasn't. Baby Jesus evidenced no trouble at all with either Latin or Greek.

We read Milton together, finding pleasure in certain passages. We reenacted the Restoration dramas. She was Lady Teazle.

She brought me mice she'd dispatched.

She loved me. I needed that. Some people like to proclaim they don't need anyone, they don't need love. They come a cropper. Sooner or later those deluded, egotistical "loners" come home by Weeping Cross. We all need one another. I knew I needed love, most especially from cats, dogs, and horses.

We'd go down to Minetta Lane, the party part of the Village. One of the police horse stables was there, literally under the ground. Once the fellows learned I knew my way around a stable, they allowed me to groom the horses. Baby Jesus caught mice there but she had to listen to the other cats bitch and moan about her. Oh, what heaven to smell horses, leather, Absorbine, Jr., saddle soap.

I never asked to ride the horses. Most of them were crossed; many had Morgan blood, I think. No Thoroughbreds, but as Thoroughbreds often have thin coats and sensitive temperaments, this showed good judgment. In fact, the New York Police Department is quite a good department. The tarring and feathering they've endured because of some corruption is so out of proportion it infuriates me. New Yorkers are far luckier than they know to be served by such people. And the riders liked their horses. How funny, because a lot of these men (all men then) hadn't known one end of a horse from another when they were first assigned to the equine unit. They learned. They hit the ground a lot in learning, too.

Baby Jesus and I were happiest brushing, picking hooves, noticing the hoof angle the blacksmith had chosen. Learning about hooves is a lifelong study. I know the basics. A good blacksmith is as important as a good vet.

The other joy for Baby Jesus and me was our walks in Washington Square Park during the day. She wore a harness and walked on a leash. Any dog foolish enough to charge her soon sported a bloody nose.

Mother and Aunt Mimi, far away, wrote letters and I wrote back. Phone service was expensive, so you only made a phone call if someone had a baby or died. Mother wrote three letters a week on average. I managed one.

I'd made some friends, although their accents occasionally made it difficult for me to understand them. Eventually I got the hang of it.

New York University forced me to take remedial speech to eradicate my accent before they'd give me my diploma. I can talk Yankee, but as soon as I cross that Mason–Dixon Line, I speak the King's English.

Baby Jesus grew into a sleek tabby. She liked to play catch. She'd even retrieve. Once a friend who actually owned a car drove us out of the city, up into Dutchess County. James Cagney was alive then, active, owned a great big gorgeous farm. He loved horses, so my friend drove me by. Mr. Cagney was clearly a man who knew horses. How I wish I had known him. He ran an impressive operation.

New York State, formed by wide glacier swaths into a long series of ridges and hills, is just different enough from Virginia to provoke comment but similar enough to feel comfortable.

Once I graduated from New York University, I spent a couple of years in the city to take advantage of all the museums, the theater, and the grand New York Public Library at Forty-second and Fifth. I never could sneak Baby Jesus in there. She would have liked the Celeste Bartos Room. Her kind of style.

The jogging craze swept New York. The cat and I thought it was funny to watch people huffing and puffing. Good for them, though. We knew it was time to leave town when we were passed on the east side of Central Park by a woman jogging in a black cashmere sweater and a simple strand of pearls.

A part-time teaching job became available at Cazenovia College in Cazenovia, New York, which is twenty-some miles east of Syracuse.

No car. Little money. One suitcase of clothing. We were ready. Baby rode in a carrying case on the train. We picked a time when there wouldn't be too many people so no one would fuss. She wasn't happy on the train, but she was elated when we reached our destination. A yard. Woods. Farms. Horses. Cattle. Deer. Real life.

It would be another decade before I could finally buy my own farm, but I was on my way. I could learn from animals again instead of just smiling at a Norwegian Elkhound being walked on a leash on a city street.

In August I noticed squirrels picking up the pace. In Virginia, August is hotter than the hinges of hell. Baby Jesus stopped shedding. By September the nights had cooled. The days, clear for the most part, couldn't have been more perfect. Usually it was in the mid-sixties. By the end of the month, a blush shone on the maple leaves and nights could even be cold. Horses' coats grew heavy. The first snow fell mid-October.

Baby and I took long walks. We could be in the country in fifteen minutes, especially if we walked toward the northwest. Wildlife needed higher calories earlier than they did back home. They needed fat on their bodies.

Weak things died fast. As much of the farmland grew corn, the gleanings helped. Nothing helped during pounding storms, blinding snow, and subzero temperatures. Those animals with the thickest coats, best dens, or most sheltered nests pulled through.

Most people put out birdseed. A few put out food for deer (this was before deer overpopulation). I put out a five-gallon bucket for foxes, with a two-inch hole drilled near the bottom. It's filled with kibble mixed with corn oil, and refilled once every two weeks in bad weather.

This magnolia blossom isn't meant to live where the mercury sinks to twenty below. I gained respect for the people and animals who endured it. Some may even enjoy it. What with the layers of clothing, the heating bills for nearly eight months, the extra tending to your vehicle, Upstate New York sucked the salary right out of my pocket. What winter didn't filch, that greedy state government did. New York folks pay outrageous taxes and most of it slides down to New York City. Why the residents of Upstate New York don't march on Albany I will never figure out.

Another thing I noticed, and this was in 1971: fewer farm animals. People couldn't feed as many animals as we can in Virginia because the forage season is so short. If you can't make enough hay you must buy it.

If you live through winter, which ends about May (mud season), June, July, and August are spectacular.

When my term ended, fate stepped in. Hollywood called. I answered. What a jolt from Upstate New York's climate to semi-arid California. As I spent most of the day in the studio, I saw few animals other than coyotes and birds if I managed to get out for lunch.

My tour of duty finally ended and Baby Jesus and I zoomed home. Hay. Trees. Wildlife everywhere. Four distinct seasons with winter lasting three to four months. Virginia, to me, is paradise.

The richest period of my life was about to begin, and all the lessons of my youth would be intertwined with it.

My favorite opponent. I love foxes! *Photo courtesy of Bill Gamble.*

Pretty Is as Pretty Does

Horses, like women, dazzle. The result: brains fly out the window. Even experienced horsemen can lose their composure. You pay for beauty. How men can afford mistresses, I don't know. A stay-at-home wife costs plenty (not that she doesn't do her part), but if a man had to pay for all her services it would roll up the annual bill over a hundred thousand dollars. Thirty-some years ago *Ms.* magazine totted up the cost, and it would have been sixty thousand, if memory serves.

Same with a horse. A bad one costs as much as a good one to keep. As to initial purchase, that, too, can be influenced by emotion.

My farm outside Charlottesville was a piddling thirty-four acres. The barn needed work. The stall floors sported potholes that would have made a New Yorker feel right at home. This is the result of horses pawing and owners not filling in the holes and tamping them down tight. Rather than fool with potholes, I just dug out the stalls three feet down and releveled them. At the bottom, I put in six inches of number-five stone. That's stone about the size of a shooter marble. Helps with drainage. Over that I poured pea rock, dirt, and finally, on top, rock dust, which I watered and rolled. Over all this I put a layer of masonry sand. Rolled that, too. Six stalls gave me a good workout. If I could rent five and provide care, I figured I could own my first horse.

The farm, tidy and bright, showed well, as a real estate agent might put it. I hung out my shingle and in one week I had those five stalls filled. I had put up new fencing, the paddocks were spacious, and the pastures were in pretty good order. Naturally, one overseeds every autumn. At least if you're smart in central Virginia you do because our climate swings wildly, not just in terms of temperature but in terms of rainfall. Central Virginia is the transition between a southern climate and a northern one.

Baby Jesus, sixteen now, watched me work perched on a bench in the garden. Her sidekick was a Great Dane puppy, black as coal, named India Ink. I never had to train the puppy. Baby Jesus did it for me. India was one of the best-behaved dogs I've ever known. I can't say the same for Baby, as she was a tyrant.

Once the boarders were in the barn she'd saunter down, not a trace of arthritis, visit each stall, and hiss great big hisses. Then she'd turn and saunter out.

The horses blinked. A few stopped chewing hay to study the skinny old cat with the luminous green eyes. Occasionally, she'd climb one of the support beams and drop down onto a stall door. The old boards, thick oak, would cost a fortune today. Back then it was castoff lumber. The boards rose up to five feet. Above that, a mesh screen made of wire about half the width of your little finger separated the stalls. Wouldn't do to have one horse reach over to take a hunk out of another. Even horses born together can get into it, and my boarders had to learn to get along with one another.

Baby would drop onto the stall door just to prove she could do it. Her chest swelled with pride if she scared the occupant enough to bolt to a corner or run outside (I usually opened the back door of the stall so they could come and go as they pleased). If they needed larger turnout, I'd walk them to one of the big pastures.

India tagged along, falling over her giant paws. This always elicited a snotty comment from Baby, whose tail would stand straight up as she delivered her sarcasm.

I knew hardly a soul. Sure, I knew a few merchants, but I mean real friends. Baby, India, and the boarders were my buddies. I did know one friend from high school. However, he had two small children, taught full time, and was on overload. Still, it was nice to know I could pick up the phone if necessary.

He told me who the reputable horse dealers were and whom to avoid. If you think about it, the horse business is the original used car business. Lucky for me, I knew something about horses. I knew enough to stop myself from buying a great beauty who had a screw loose. Instead, I bought a horse that was so ugly he made your eyes water. A bay of nondescript breeding with a common clunky head, he needed groceries to put some meat on his bones. He had an old low bow on his left foreleg, little knots and windpuffs on the others. I liked him. He was a survivor. The vet listed his blemishes but told me what I hoped to hear: he was serviceably sound. I looked at X-rays of his front hooves (always a good idea when you're buying a horse) and he was okay.

A word of caution here: You can read perfectly clean X-rays and the horse can be dead lame the next day. On the other hand, you can read X-rays that horsemen say have "changes" and learn an important thing or two. You might see the beginning of navicular or other conditions affecting the hoof or the bones just above it. Think of the horse's hoof area as somewhat analogous to the bones in your wrist. Not a perfect parallel, but it will give you an idea. When a horse jumps, the pressure per square inch on the foreleg and those bones is tremendous. It is when you jump, too.

This fellow was ten and he had no name, or none that anyone could remember. I called him Major and I owe him a great deal. For one thing, he tolerated Baby Jesus, even neighing to her. She'd saunter (Baby rarely walked—it was always the Mae West saunter) to the fence line, where she'd climb a post and wait for Major to trot over to her. Then she'd rub against his face. That hateful cat just loved Major. It was mutual. They had the longest chats. I'd see them together when I went in to muck the stalls, and when I was finished, forty-five minutes later (I have a good speedy system plus the good stall floor helped), I'd find them in the same spot, still thrilled silly with each other's company. Meanwhile, the ever-growing India stayed underfoot. What a sweet, sweet dog.

My boarders paid on time. They rode around the farm and loaded up their horses to foxhunt, usually with Farmington Hunt, though one boarder hunted with Keswick. Albemarle County is one of the few counties in America to host two foxhunts, both very good and therefore very competitive with each other. Each pushes the other onward and upward. As Keswick was founded in 1886 it can look upon Farmington, founded in 1929, as an upstart. Each club has had wonderful masters, and a few who should have stayed in bed. And each club has a well-mounted first flight with people who can ride and ride hard.

I'd wistfully watch my boarders drive off. I was dying to hunt and I knew Major could do it because he had the jumping gene. I needed a lot more work than he did. Still do. One must always keep learning, keep the legs strong and the hands soft.

To hunt I'd need a truck, at least a three-quarter-ton, a trailer, and the money to pay for the gas. My vehicle was an old red

Toyota truck that rattled the fillings right out of your head. It was distinctive since my neighbor's goat had once feasted on the interior.

One of my boarders, a giant fellow with a booming voice, Dr. Jimmy Turner, invited me to hunt with him and his wife, Alice. They loaded up Major, hauled me to a Farmington fixture—a fixture is a specific place where one hunts; a fortunate club has many fixtures—and Jimmy being Jimmy, he paid my cap fee, fussing terribly when I attempted to repay him. I rode second flight, fearing I'd make a fool of myself in first flight. Plus, when first flight contains people like Ellie Wood Keith Baxter, who won the Medal McClay in 1937 and also won at Madison Square Garden before World War II and again after, I had good reason to be scared. Eventually I moved up and, of course, provided hilarity for all.

Major took care of me. I'm much more of an athlete than a rider. I'd never had a riding lesson but I had balance. I didn't care how stupid I looked or how ugly my horse: I was in heaven. A few people deigned to nod toward me. Pat Butterfield, now Master of Foxhounds there, who was my high school friend, and his wife, Kay (another hell of a horseman), Jane Fogelman, and Gloria Fennell all welcomed me.

My boarders paid my horse expenses and a bit of the mortgage; the farm wasn't very expensive. But I just couldn't swing the truck, the trailer, and Farmington's annual fees. All far beyond what I could do. I had no job. I'd come back with what I'd saved from Hollywood, which was a lot since I lived close to the bone out there, investing my earnings in real estate, which paid off.

Here I was, thirty-one, at the prime of my life, I thought (wrong—my prime is right now, and I'm not kidding), watching every penny, working from sunup to long after sundown. Loved that. Can't work outside enough. I had a quarter-acre garden full of sweet corn, white corn, asparagus, you name it. I thought I'd earn a little off the crops, and did. The asparagus was snapped up before I could even cart it to the outdoor market.

Still.

Baby Jesus suggested I write another novel. Something with sex and violence. I did. *High Hearts,* set during the War Between the States. Enough money came in that I could finally buy a truck and trailer. I met Art Bushey, the Ford dealer, who was, and still is, crazy (in a good way). I loved him, of course. Art made sure that that truck could pull a house off its foundations. I bought a dually instead of a three-quarter-ton truck on his advice. He was right as rain. That extra set of wheels can save your hindquarters, and your horse's, too, should you drop a wheel over the edge of an uneven road. Kept the old Toyota since I'd have gotten only five hundred dollars in trade. That truck breathed its last when 300,000 clicked over on the odometer. And it wasn't the engine that died. The body just rusted out. Japanese steel is better now. Used to be cheap crap.

My beloved Major did not ride in the two-horse gooseneck trailer until I could back up with no problems and take a tight turn. Finally, I loaded him up and off we trundled to another FHC hunt. Most hunts allow three caps a year. This was my second. What a corker. Second flight was led by Dr. Herbert Jones. This was the first time I saw the man who was to become my best friend, my moral compass, my second skin. Foxfield was the fixture. What a glorious day, filled with crisp, long runs. Herb put us in the right place every time. I've never seen so many foxes or a man so commanding without appearing to command. Herb had women fall over him throughout his life, even when he ran to fat (which I so kindly pointed out to him daily). I joined "Herbie's Harem."

Major seemed amused by all this. He loved hunting. His ears swiveled to capture the hounds' voices, the horn. He always saw the fox before I did. If I bobbled, he managed to shift to that side.

Jimmy Turner's youngest teenage daughter, Doodles, started giving me lessons. Thank God. And when she went back to high school, I landed on Muffin Barnes's doorstep at Gloria Fennell's barn. Poor Muffin. She did her best, and over time it paid off. I have the Barnes leg. She gives you a really strong, good leg and it has saved my nether regions on countless occasions.

Money concerns eased up. Hollywood is a strange place. If you're available, they don't want you. Remove yourself and everyone wants you. I'd fly out, pick up a movie of the week to write, fly home, and then deliver it. Meanwhile, my novels would climb onto that "New York Times Extended Best-Seller List."

Major now had everything a horse could want. Beautiful English leather tack, a bridle with a sewn-in bit, a Baker blanket, a cooler, carrots, peppermint candies (his fave).

India and Major got along fine, but Baby Jesus was the horse's boon companion. Sometimes as I'd walk up toward the house she'd linger, coming up with the fireflies. He'd nicker goodnight.

This friendship deepened. But Baby had years on her, and at eighteen her health took a turn for the worse. I would carry her down for her sessions with Major. He knew, of course, and he'd place his muzzle on her flank but wouldn't push. The day came when I knew I'd have to put her down, and the most wonderful small animal vet, Chuck Wood, actually drove out to my farm so she wouldn't have to be frightened by the drive or the smells of his office. What a kind man. She did not leave this earth peacefully, I might add. Tyrannical to the end. When Chuck came through the kitchen door she tried to escape, and then she was not easily held. She so wanted to live, but her systems were shutting down. The greater cruelty would have been to pump her up with steroids or whatever for a day or two. It really was time.

That cat loved me when I lived on five dollars a week in New York City, when we slept rolled up in blankets with my old pea jacket thrown over us for extra warmth. She now sits on the top left shelf by the fireplace in my workroom in a Thai funerary urn in the shape of a red cat. When I go down, Baby is going with me. We'll be commingled ashes.

I thought about taking the body to Major so he could smell her but decided against it. He watched as I buried her under the weeping cherry tree. He knew anyway. When I moved to the big farm where I now live I disinterred her and had what was left cremated.

How he mourned. He dropped weight. His eyes lost their luster. I did my best to keep him in shape, and God bless him, he did what I asked. Finally, I turned him out to heal in his own time.

A month after Baby Jesus died, a pregnant stray wound up in the barn. The result: a pregnant stray now enjoyed the benefits of health care and proper nutrition. Four beautiful kittens came into this world. I kept all of them.

I'd made a whelping box in the tack room. The mother cat wasn't suited for house life. I could catch her, with difficulty, but she wanted to be in the barn. One day I opened the door to Major's stall after he'd walked in from his back door. He stepped out, stopped, opened his nostrils wide, then walked to the tack room. He ducked his head inside. The kittens, eyes now open, were wobbly. The mother wasn't at all sure about this big boy.

She was transfixed. Major didn't move. So I just worked around him, then put him back.

He picked up weight. He always wanted to visit the kittens, and as they grew older, out they tumbled into the center aisle. Once they turned eight weeks old I brought them up to the house. India knew her place where cats were concerned. No problems there, plus they knew one another from barn visits.

Every morning, the kittens would follow me back down to the barn. The mother cat struck up a friendship with Major. He was getting a few years on him, too, but he came back strong, and when fall rolled around, we applied for membership at Farmington. There is a trial period. We both passed.

Love does work miracles. It's such a hackneyed thing to say but it's true. Once people experience it, they no longer snicker behind their hand or roll their eyes that one could be so sentimental.

Pretty is as pretty does. Major took care of me. He taught me, as each of my animals does in one form or another, the power of love. But he also taught me the power of birth and rebirth. The kittens brought him back to life.

Should you be reading this, if you've gone through a deep loss, be patient. Like Major, you'll be reborn. Some of your friends may not understand if the love of an animal pulls you through or brings you back to life, but I do. And Major would, too.

Here I'm riding Silver Investor, hounds packing in to first cast. I'm doing what I love most in the world, hunting my hounds on a good horse.
Photo by Cynthia Green Photography.

The Thrill of the Hunt

A life well lived is one filled with pleasures. Troubles and pain find each of us, and it's up to us to find our own delights. For me, these exist in nature. The Metropolitan Museum of Art delivers pleasure for a time, and the same is true of the theater. But eventually the crowds begin to wear on me.

H. L. Mencken defined Puritanism as "the haunting fear that someone, somewhere, may be happy." Good description. That type of personality exists all over the globe among humankind. Animals aren't that stupid. Unfortunately, in some parts of England and the United States north of the Mason-Dixon Line, Puritan qualities—prudence, thrift, sobriety—are valued above other fine attributes. The Protestant work ethic is hallowed. Poor sods.

Apart from those who have inherited wealth (a curse as well as a blessing), we all must work. I suppose we make a virtue of necessity. For me, it's necessity. I like my work but I like hunting better. I feel most alive outside, flying along or walking along studying the brush for tufts of fur, small spirals of feathers, scat. Foxhunting is the grand passion of my life.

Again, Americans don't kill the fox. If a fox is old or sick, yes, it is dispatched, but in the last seventeen years, I've had that happen three times. The English kill. Their agricultural practices differ from ours and their enclosure laws have created a nation of lovely squares and rectangles. Not so here. Cultivation over large areas came late to our part of the world—no Roman invasions to begin the process over two thousand years ago. Good news for wild creatures, especially the fox. There are dens in which to disappear, fallen logs to jump up on and lift one's scent, the dens of other animals to pop into in a pinch. And you can always hop in the back of a station wagon, which I saw a fox do in the late 1980s when a lady had the tailgate of her Wagoneer down. Fox hopped right in as she motored slowly away.

Hunting sharpens my senses, for I must use each of them. The people who come out in all weather add spice to the process. The hunt field isn't a place for wimps. Foxhunters are throwbacks—another reason why I love them. Physical prowess keeps you in one piece. Sooner or later you'll break a bone but they heal fast enough. I've ridden with broken ribs, separated ribs, broken nose, torn hands. Your adrenaline spikes so high you know you're hurt but you don't really feel it until later. I did feel it when a horse went over on me, but I crawled out from under, thank you, Jesus.

The acceptance of risk fades from our world. People want guarantees. Your government lies to you, brokerage houses lie to you, insurance companies lie to you. They tell you they'll remove or reduce the risk. Impossible. What government can and does do is redistribute the pain depending upon who is in power.

Foxhunters accept risk. I won't go so far as to say we court it like a bungee jumper.

The images you see of foxhunting usually involve horses at a gallop, people on their backs in varying states of grace, and a lovely pack of hounds forward. In reality, you often walk or trot for an hour or more, depending on conditions, before you move on. You can smell the earth if it's not frozen, the leaves on the ground as they pulverize, the scent of other animals if your nose is good. Up in the sky you'll see sundogs glinting. Once a group of us were walking back from a long hunt in early March and we caught a rare sight. Slashes of turquoise crossed the sky at one in the afternoon. It was as if one of the gods had taken a crayon and marked up the heavens. The turquoise was so vivid it stood out against a backdrop of robin's egg blue and the white clouds. Other times you'll cast your eyes west, sun on your face, to see gunmetal gray clouds piling up behind the Blue Ridge Mountains. A thin cloud cover soon obscures the sun. Swirls and streams of snow slide down the eastern slope of those fabled mountains. In ten to twenty minutes, depending on the speed of the clouds, the snow will fall on my farm. The fox knows that the snow is coming long before you or I see the clouds. By the time we do, she is snug in her den, tail curled over that black nose.

Everyone needs a passion, something that won't bring you money, something on which to spend a bit of money, something sublimely impractical, capable of stirring your emotions. Watching your favorite football team can stir your emotions, but you are sitting on your can. Better to keep moving. For some it's golf. For others it's gardening.

Such a passion often brings people to good deeds. For instance, many foxhunters are involved in animal rescue, including horses, which are difficult to place and expensive to bring back to health. But we do it because those wonderful animals allow us to do what we love.

Deer hunters all over America contribute to organizations like Hunters for the Hungry. Somehow, our passions do lead us, most of us, to a form of giving. Or teaching young people. If those of us who farm and hunt don't pass on our skills they'll be lost by the middle of the twenty-first century. For me, this is a terrifying thought.

We are medium-size predators. Farming is perhaps ten thousand years old, maybe a bit older in some parts of the world, much younger in others. We survived by hunting. We learned to cooperate through hunting. To hunt is to be human. Remove this and slowly you destroy the human animal. Look at what has happened to certain breeds of dogs in the show world. There is no way they can perform the functions for which they were first bred. The AKC has awakened to this threat, as have many of the breed organizations. Extinction, or the diminishing of some wonderful, irreplaceable species, can and will happen if we don't wake up.

Foxhunting has taught me to cooperate with my horse, the hounds, and other humans. It has also forced me to confront the dangers of untrammeled development. Once concrete is laid over the corn you won't eat from those acres again and neither will any other life form. From the 1950s onward, suburbanization has gobbled up productive land, created traffic problems, and forced taxes to be raised to pay for services to those developments. I'm opposed to environmentally unsound development.

Foxes, being omnivorous, can and do live in cities. More live in the suburbs. The fox and I, however, flourish in the country. I have noticed an affinity for churchyards for both of us.

I don't think animals have an impulse toward religion, yet they appear to have affiliations. There's a fox in Nelson County, Virginia, who is a careless Protestant. The above-mentioned fox keeps a den near Trinity Episcopal Church, displaying little interest in the service or parishioners. However, only a mile down the road reposes the small, abandoned, but lovely St. Mary's Chapel.

A succession of gray foxes have lived there for the last seventeen years, probably longer. As I am directly across the road about twice a month from October to March, I have had occasion to observe their practices. The Hollands, owners of Oak Ridge, have not been able to purchase the chapel, which was once a part of the estate. It sits exposed. John Holland does his best to protect it. Mr. Tyree, former manager of Oak Ridge, now in his high eighties, does his best, too. But out from under John and Rhonda Holland's protective umbrella one can only expect so much, and occasionally the door will be forced open. When times are bad, as they now are, homeless people have sought shelter there. No heat—but it is a roof over your head. Heather Goodwin, the Hollands' oldest daughter, helps run the estate. I know preservation of the church concerns her and her husband, too.

Once I parked my horse trailer at the church only to be chastised by a descendant of Thomas Fortune Ryan (he who made Oak Ridge what it is today, which is to say stupendous) for parking there. The descendant was visiting from New York, I think. Our hunt club also does its best to protect the chapel because it has deep meaning for us, a few of us being Catholic and the rest of us adoring the gray fox of St. Mary's. City people have a hard time imagining why people who have no financial interest in a structure will care for the property. Money, money, money. If we aren't being paid, how could we possibly care? In short, we were trespassing. So I no longer look out for St. Mary's. I don't go where I'm not wanted.

But I still care for the fox. She gets her kibble with wormer once a month. When pregnant, no wormer, obviously, and none until the cubs reach close to six months. One Christmas I left my old rosary beads at her den because Mrs. Mary Tattersall O'Brien,

M.D., had given me a new set of silver rosary beads. Quite a present. Later, I checked for my old beads. The fox had pulled them into her den.

Foxes like pretty things almost the way blackbirds do. Maybe that's why the Catholic fox stays by the chapel. Despite all, beauty lingers, and every now and then I can't resist. I'll ring the bell, tidings of joy for a beautiful day, robust health, wily foxes, willing hounds, and kind horses. There's so much to celebrate. When I can't contain my happiness I have noticed a pair of eyes peeping out at me. She likes the bell, too. She likes what I bring to her after a hunt even better, for we always have a tailgate. The Catholic fox occasionally cooperates and gives us a run. The Episcopal fox only does so if he's jumped coming back late from a hunt. Years ago, I did surprise him. He's a big red. I picked him up on the other side of the racetrack. Mrs. Hazel Wright, still alive then, delighted in having us hunt her land, which sits smack in the middle of Oak Ridge. Until the last two decades of her life—she was close to a hundred when she died—one of our members would bundle her up and walk her out so she could listen. Her sight was gone by then. Whoever inherited this duty then heard all her hunting stories, and she had stored up quite a collection. I miss her.

The Episcopal fox, down in an old barn that was maybe a mile west of the house by the farm roads, must have fallen asleep on a full stomach. All this land lies south of Oak Ridge's abovementioned wonderful racetrack. The horn awakened him and he shot out of that barn like a bat out of hell. What a run, straight as an arrow. We had to negotiate a less than perfect coop in the fence line by the racetrack. A coop is an attractive jump built into a fence line, so named because it resembles a big chicken coop. We stayed on the outside of the track. His tail was straight out, his stride stretched to the fullest. What a glorious sight. Foxes are fast. The hounds closed in, keeping about ten yards behind. He crossed the macadam road. No traffic—we breathed a collective sigh of relief. The choir boomed from Trinity; we could hear the hymn. The fox disappeared, either into the graveyard or perhaps into a den by the foundation. I couldn't find out because the hounds were considering joining the service. And in full cry. The field—the people following the hounds on horseback—had the great good sense to pull up on the east side of the church by the graveyard.

I couldn't blow my horn or I'd disturb the service, but I had to retrieve my hounds. Dr. Mary (our nickname for Dr. Mary O'Brien) was way on the other side of the racetrack where she should have been. My other whipper-in, Dana Flaherty, a Lutheran, was laughing so hard she just about fell off her horse. In other words, she was useless at that exact moment.

I quietly called my hounds, some of whom entered the vestibule. A few canine heads turned my way, but the singing inside Trinity thrilled them. Some of them stepped out of the vestibule to find that smart fox. Finally, after pleading, I managed to extract the remainder. The minister, a marvelous soul who blesses our hounds on opening hunt, Rev. Judy Parrish, saw fit not to fly out and deliver a blessing of another sort. I was never so glad to ride away from a place in my life. Those of us who lived through that incident occasionally recall it.

This Episcopal fox lacks Christian charity. We picked him up two years later heading out of the graveyard. He barreled straight to Route 29, a four-lane highway heavily traveled, and ducked into a culvert under the road. Some of my hounds crossed the road. No one was hurt. I blew my horn and held the rest of the pack, and John Morris, Jr. wheel whip (meaning he's in the truck), laid rubber getting around to that spot, which was a good two miles from where I was in the meadows. Thank God, the hounds returned to the horn. Snow lay on the ground. I shivered a bit as I counted heads. "All on" means all your hounds are together, and they were. Except for Juno.

Later that night, Mr. Wright (no relation to Hazel) called to tell me he had found Juno dead among his cattle, not a mark on her. John picked her up and we buried her, with difficulty. We needed a pickax to dig, for the ground was like concrete. It could be she died of shock from having been hit by a car. I still mourn Juno, for she was a terrific hound bursting with Bywaters blood, a line I prize. But Juno was naughty about returning to the horn. She'd keep hunting until it suited her to stop. Much as I miss her, and she was a beauty as well, she reminded me of this old piece of wisdom: Don't keep a hound if he or she doesn't listen to you or your horn. The foxhunting word to describe an obedient hound is "biddable." So in foxhunting terms: Don't keep a hound that isn't biddable.

I avoid the Episcopal fox. Murder rests in his heart. Even the good words of "Father Judy" (I tease Rev. Parrish thus) don't soften his attitude.

As for the Catholic fox, I saw her last week when I cruised through Oak Ridge. Her children are dispersing to form dens of their own. One—I'm pretty sure it's hers—lives in front of the grand estate, sunning himself and cavorting, mostly to amuse the Hollands.

When I first saw Oak Ridge in the early 1970s there was a tree growing up through the breakfast room and out through the roof. How sad to see such grandeur fallen to ruin. It's all restored now. Back then, I also found a family of black foxes. They're grays, really, but so dark they look black. To this day, Oak Ridge has black foxes; they have traveled as far as Mrs. Anne Fortune Henderson's Cherry Hill, maybe three miles away as the crow flies but further for us. They've also made it all the way to the Upper James River, for I have seen them at the Old Norwood estate. How beautiful they are. I have also seen one that was raised as a pet. I was driving and saw him walking along. I stopped to pick him up, then noticed the collar with a nameplate on it. This was a good ten years ago, but that was one happy fox.

My hounds are Episcopalian. For close to fourteen years, the Reverend Daniel Wheeler blessed them. He passed away Saturday, October 4, 2008. Although a Baptist, he never chided the hounds for their Episcopalian affiliation. Possessed of a voice that could herald angels, when he blessed them, all those hound heads, and horses, too, turned to face him, ears forward, eyes bright. The hounds loved him. You can tell when hounds favor someone, and Reverend Wheeler was beloved. For years he headed a church and we would all contribute as a thank-you for the blessing. After he retired, he simply wouldn't take a penny. "Feed the hounds," he'd say with a smile.

Now, most of you know that an unemployed minister is hardly a millionaire. Rev. Wheeler's generosity touched all of us who were staff. His son, David, is one of my Joint Masters. Bob Satterfield, he of the deadly charm, is the other.

When David called to tell me his dad had left us, I went to the hounds. My grandfather and great-uncle told me whenever someone hounds love passes, you must tell them. This is also true of bees. You must go to the hive.

The hounds know. How? I don't know. The usual excitement that greets me every time I go to my children was subdued. They live with me but on the other side of the creek. I can walk to the kennels in seven minutes. I sat with them to inform them of our loss. We considered how lucky we all were to know such a man and his family. Good people. His wife, a great beauty whom age has not dimmed, was married to him for sixty-odd years. His daughter, Rosemary, by the way, looks just like her mother, a real head-turner. Hounds understand fidelity, love, and kindness. David and his siblings, Marion, Rosemary, and Tim, share these traits.

Three years ago I named a wriggly puppy Wheeler for Rev. Wheeler. Now a full-grown hound, he's a whopping seventy-five pounds at least, and quite noticeable in the field. He's just coming into his own. He hunted the Sunday after Rev. Wheeler's call to glory. He hunted the best he's ever hunted in his life. The Reverend Daniel Wheeler would have been proud.

On December 21, 2007, I was also given a reminder of how animals know when someone they love has gone on. Al Toews (pronounced Tays) was Master of Bassets of Ashland Bassets in Warrenton, Virginia, about an hour and a half north of my farm. Al, a combat helicopter pilot in Vietnam, was a good hound man. Like most men who have actually fought in a war he never paraded his masculinity. He was a real man, and the hounds responded to his authenticity. Hunting hounds wasn't natural to Al. He had to learn, and he did so pretty much as he'd learned to fly helicopters, by breaking everything down into sequences. He became a good huntsman and a good hound breeder, importing Gascon Bleus from France for an infusion to his pack, a masterstroke. Sometimes when hunting he lacked the patience of his Joint Master, Mary Reed, who now hunts the hounds and is a natural. Both Mary and I, in those few minutes we snatch to catch up, talk about how much we learned from Al precisely because he wasn't a natural. He left volumes of notes and clippings, which his widow, Kathleen King, is wrestling into shape when she isn't struggling with the aftermath. Al, a stubborn man, didn't leave a will. A week before he died he said he'd make one and then boom, there went his heart.

This story leads back to my hounds, but first I have tell you a little more about Al. He was a true introvert, as am I, the difference being that I had cotillion so you'd never know. Al, from Nebraska, never heard of cotillion until he landed, literally, in Virginia. He and I—well, for me it was love at first sight. I simply adored him, a common response among women. Kathleen endured it. Al hadn't a clue. Women and hounds loved him. He preferred hounds.

He drafted (gave) me four bassets to start my pack: Leah, Luciano (her son), Robin, and the aptly named Outlaw. From them I bred two litters. Two years later, the day Al died, I walked into their kennel to feed, clean, and exercise the bassets. This is an afternoon chore, as the foxhounds are worked in the morning. So it's the close of my working day and I look forward to it. The youngsters bounced up, but Leah, Luciano, Robin, and Outlaw looked as though they'd eaten poison. Listless, depressed, no appetite. For a basset not to have an appetite is frightening. They'll eat you out of house and home. They can be at death's door yet still pig out. I took their temperatures, checked gums; they seemed okay. Worried though I was, I've been around animals long enough to know that you shouldn't panic. Unless you know it's serious or you see the injury, wait a bit before calling the vet. It's the equivalent of taking an aspirin and calling the doctor in the morning.

Dr. Mary worked with dogs while in medical school. She's used to my frequent queries and is always gracious about it. I went inside to call her, picked up the phone, and got the message beep. Kathleen had left a message that Al had just died of a heart attack while driving his truck. A pilot to the end, he got it off the road so as not to harm anyone else. How this man did that in excruciating pain I will never know. He was a warrior. The four hounds knew before I did because Al trained and hunted them for years. I hurried back out, sat with Leah and Robin, petted the boys. We helped one another but it took a good two weeks for them to return to their ebullient selves.

The bassets, I'm pretty sure, are Catholic, although Al was not. There's a touch of Rome about them. They adore ritual and adornment, and they wait for me to issue papal bulls. Only, with them I suspect they emphasize the bull.

Animals feel and they feel deeply, some more than others, just like some people. That they know about death before we do is a mystery. And yet I have friends who have told me that when someone they loved passed away, they woke up to see the departed in their room or felt that the figure had come to their desk at work. They were surprised, scared in some cases, when they found out that the visitation occurred at the loved one's time of death.

I am not blinded by science. I don't need answers for much of what I don't know. That I observe and feel is enough for me. I fear we are hag-ridden by logic, losing spontaneous beauty and wisdom. I trust my senses. I trust myself. Those animals that love you *know*. They also know when you're sick, often before you do. I trust my animals, on many levels, more than I trust myself.

Anyone who thinks animals don't have emotions is a blistering idiot. I'll give ground on religion. Maybe my St. Mary's fox doesn't really care for mass, but does she feel, can she be weary with sorrow, leap for joy? You bet. While I don't think my foxes have read the Bible, there is a passage they follow religiously: "Make a joyful noise unto the Lord." They sure do. And we should, too.

Sneaky Pie, not taking her duties seriously. I think she's been hitting the catnip. Is there a Betty Ford for cats? *Photo by Cindy Chandler.*

A Bicycle Built for Two

Cats love us despite our being human. Dogs love us because we're human. Perhaps they wish to guide us, if we would only listen.

People ask me which I love more—cats or dogs. How can I possibly answer? That's like being asked which of your children you love the most. The best you can say is that each child possesses different qualities but your love remains constant.

An odd thing about long, abiding love is that it's often hard to remember where and when it all started. My business partner is a cat, Sneaky Pie. On Saint Francis's Day, October 4, forget the exact year in the 1980s, I visited the SPCA with a friend, Ruth Dalksy, who was looking for her lost dog. The Albemarle County SPCA was crowded with adults and children waiting for the priest to bless their animal friends, which made looking for Ruth's dog harder. We had to push through people to examine the dog runs. Finally, I drew back to stand in front of the cat cages, one crate stacked on the next. A little paw reached out and grabbed the back of my head. Untangling my hair from those tiny claws I turned around to look into gorgeous green eyes. A lifelong friendship followed. If only I'd had the room at that time to take her sister and her mother. I've often prayed that someone else adopted them. Sneaky grew into a sleek gray tabby. She liked to ride in the truck. Many of my cats jump into the truck as eagerly as the dogs do. In her case, she had to stand on the seat, paws on the dash, and drive with you. She rarely took her eyes off the road.

Whether we were born with it or developed it over time, we each knew what the other was thinking. I had a similar connection with a glorious American foxhound, Diane. Sneaky, however, could be tart. Diane was always sweet.

The name Sneaky Pie comes from an old Southern expression. When you watch a person put one over on another person or they do it to you directly (assuming it doesn't make you mad or cost you a lot of money), you might say, "Why, you old sneaky pie!"

Tiny as she was when I brought her back to the farm, the kitten exuded all the wiles of Odysseus. Here was a trickster. She'd catch frogs, careful not to puncture their innards, and put them in the dog's water bucket. The frog could get out if the water nearly touched the rim, otherwise it would swim until it died of exhaustion. I usually found them in time, but it scared the bejesus out of the dog. Why, I don't know. The pond was full of frogs.

She'd taunt the geese at the pond. That worked until one day a large white female lost her patience and chased the cat all the way up to the house. Geese can be fierce. They've chased my cats, my dogs, even the horses. They've never chased me because I bought food for them. When the last one expired, it seemed prudent not to reintroduce such aggression.

Visitors would come. We'd sit on the porch on a hot day. In she'd dash, mouse, mole, or vole in her jaws. The benighted victim would scream and the guest would come undone. Then I'd have to rescue the little bugger without getting bitten.

How did Sneaky know which of my guests were especially

squeamish? The de-tailed skinks (a kind of lizard with an electric blue stripe on the body like a racing car) elicited screams of horror and disgust. Once she drug in a baby bunny, comatose with fear, and my guest, a nice man from the city, nearly passed out. After I tended to my guest, I removed the tiny furball from the jaws of death and managed to nurse it back to health. In a sturdy wire cage, I might add.

My Corgi, Bandit—what a buoyant spirit—and Juts, the Chow, named after my mother, lived happily with Miss Pie as long as they obeyed her every whim. If not, the howls were awful. Blood dotted the carpet from deeply scratched noses. She could be as tyrannical as Baby Jesus. I brought her a little friend, an adorable stray kitten, Pewter. The gray kitten would approach and Sneaky would turn her back. After four months, Sneaky deigned to recognize the kitty. Ultimately they became great friends, their one bone of contention being catnip.

She liked horses. She liked gardening so long as she didn't have to pull weeds. What a good bug killer, though.

When I returned to Hollywood to work for Norman Lear, she and Pewter came along. A dear friend kept the dogs until my return. She hated Hollywood because she couldn't play outside. Who was happier once home in Virginia, me or Sneaky? Pewter could be happy anywhere as long as the food was good.

Sneaky saved me. The Writers Guild struck in 1988, an eight-month, almost nine-month strike. You couldn't work. I could write novels, but Hollywood money is fast money. Novel money is slow money. The bills filled the mailbox. I paid them but cash dwindled.

One day at the typewriter, Sneaky, who was perched on the other side of the desk, looked up into my eyes and pulled down the paper. The Mrs. Murphy mystery series began.

She'd always follow me into the workroom. She stayed until each chapter was finished. She'd sink her fangs into the edge of the papers.

My agent, Wendy Weil, sold that first Mrs. Murphy to Bantam. Publishers, wonderful people for the most part, sit where they sit because they are left-brain people. If they were right-brain, they'd be doing what I do or what a painter, musician, choreographer, composer does. If you've produced A they can't grasp that you have just produced B or that it might sell. How Wendy sold the first Sneaky Pie I don't know, but she did. And for very little money, I might add. We're coming up on our eighteenth volume.

Sneaky threw herself into the series. I'd watch her. The ideas she gave me. Much as I'd derided genre literature, I ate my words. I truly clicked my heels, and best of all, I had a partner. I could talk to her, rub her head, listen intently to the cascade of meows. Her cat capers, her killings of vermin and the occasional bird (not appreciated by me) pushed me in the right direction. There's a nasty bluejay in the series based on reality. The cat's view of the world is as accurate as I can manage without being a cat. It's not exactly cute, either.

We began to make money. Thank you, Jesus. Thank you, Sneaky Pie. Thank you, Writers Guild. Without the strike the cat and I might never have formed our team.

I borrowed a bicycle built for two. What a wonderful author's photo. Since Sneaky, now a fuller-figured gray tabby but never fat (Pewter, on the other hand, became quite round), liked to ride in the car, I thought if I put her in the front basket of the bicycle built for two and I rode on the rear seat it would make an accurate photo of the relationship. She wouldn't stay in the basket. I put food in there, her favorite dried treats. No. I tried catnip. No. After three hours of diva behavior, I gave up. The photographer, flown down by Bantam, was fit to be tied. The next day he came up with a photo in the house where I was on the floor and she was leaning against me from behind. Her cooperation, illusory, lasted long enough to get the shot. My assistant at the time, all-around good guy Gordon Reistrup, was actually lying behind me holding her up. She was hateful to him after that but she eventually got over it.

People would laugh in interviews when I'd say she really was my writing partner. I never pressed it, but she was. I actually bought her a computer, a Gateway. Let me add here that I do not use computers. I never will. I value my eyes far too much. But I bought her a disc of different bird types and Gordon would load it. She sat and watched once. Then she walked outside to watch the birds live and in concert. She preferred reality to entertainment even if the birds on the disc actually were birds in life and thus filmed. She knew the difference.

She lived to almost twenty. She became thin but would still play. She came to work religiously. One morning she walked out the front door never to return. At that point coyotes had not invaded Virginia. I doubt anything snatched her. She chose to go off and die by herself. There's dignity in that.

Poor Pewter. She searched for Sneaky for days, and I searched with her. Finally we gave up. Pewter lived until one week before her twenty-third birthday.

Today, Sneaky Pie II performs the work. Her real name is Ibid. If you remember your Latin, that's "same as above." Pewter II is Gracie, and both cats look like their predecessors. However, Ibid's personality differs from her mother's. Shy and watchful, she runs from strangers. But she'll lurk nearby and I swear she's spying. Gracie, on the other hand, lives to be the center of attention.

Sneaky Pie signed her contracts along with me. Fuzzy pawprints, dipped in stamp ink, appear below my signature. She wouldn't ride the bicycle built for two but she was a true business partner. Quite tight with her money, too.

The biggest lesson she taught me, among many, is that an animal can make money. Keep your eyes and ears open. Some four-footed creature or bird friend of yours might have the answer to that terrible truth of your life: there's too much month at the end of the money.

My beloved Idler, in old age. *Photo by Cynthia Green Photography.*

Wisdom

Life is like a roll of toilet paper; the closer you get to the end the faster it goes. Wonder if it's the same for our animals, or do they remain blissfully unaware of the pages flying off the calendar? Certainly they understand they are aging, whereas I still think I'm invincible. The mind knows differently but the heart says "Go for it." In many ways my body is better than it was in my twenties. I'm stronger, faster, and know how to use it better. However, all those injuries collected during flag football, rugby, intercollegiate tennis, more rugby, and most of all polo, remind me when I wake up in the morning that I have collected a lot of "jewelry" and not from Tiffany. But one takes a hot shower, powers down some I-vitamins (ibuprofen), and soon enough, all is well.

As my animals have aged, they, too, receive supplements, extra care. The people that work for me and with me have a lot of collected wisdom. There's John Morris, Sr.; Junior "Toot," his handsome son; Robert Steppe, whom I love to torment. They can all give injections, mix potions, and bind wounds, and, if necessary and it's not bad enough for the vet, we can stitch a creature up. However, no one sews a tight stitch like a good veterinarian. I am well served by Dr. May for the small animals and Anne Bonda for the horses. John's cousin Melvin Morris works on weekends, and he's not too squeamish, either. We keep everyone feeling young.

The hunt horses range from four years old (still young) to eighteen. The eighteen-year-old bucks like a four-year-old. Everyone is in rude good health, including me, for which I am thankful.

You and I may not realize how lucky we are. Health is wealth. This is brought forcefully home when someone you love suffers or dies from a lingering disease. Sudden death is shocking, knocks you straight off your feet with grief, but to watch someone you love, human or animal, die by degrees is a special anguish.

Another form of health is in the mind. Animals can be born with mental afflictions, same as people. Much of what we deem human mental illness is a result of civilization and its discontents, to borrow a phrase from Freud. (The original neurotic, though brilliant. Ever notice how people who live from the neck up are a mess?)

Two of the lines of foxhounds I breed are slow to learn. They aren't mentally deficient, just slow. Most of my hounds are ready to learn at one and by two they really know what they're doing. But my B and C lines take an extra year. However, once they have it, you can go to the bank with them. A cousin of mine is like that, a bit slow but once it's in his brain he never forgets, and he's rock solid.

Brilliant animals, like brilliant people, make trouble if not gainfully employed. About ten years ago, I observed a remarkable animal who had correctly assessed a human's mental state.

Skyline Kennel Club was putting on a show over in Stuart's Draft. The building was a great big nondescript block containing roped rings, and there were judges for the various categories: Group I, Sporting Dogs; Group II, Hounds; Group III, Working Dogs; Group IV, Terriers; Group V, Toys; Group VI, Non-Sporting Dogs. Like all beauty pageants, the parade of pulchritude gets your blood up. The Irish Setters, like red kings and queens, commanded attention. The English Setters, more square of body, made you dream of carrying a side-by-side shotgun walking through cornfields in the fall. The bulldogs, as always, represented determination (the sweetest dogs in the kingdom, truly). The Schipperkes made you laugh. All were groomed to perfection, handled by both pros and amateurs, often the owners. Some dogs, like some people, show well. They crave the limelight. All things being equal, those are the dogs that will win a blue ribbon. When the judge picks Best in Show, so often it's a terrier due to their bright personalities.

In this kind of arena, any scent hound shows at a disadvantage, for a hound should be steady and full of drive, nose to the ground. They aren't supposed to prance out like Nureyev, head held high. In fact, I find it upsetting if they do so. A sight hound like an Afghan or Saluki shows better since they literally hunt by sight. When they can no longer see their prey, the hunt's over, whereas the foxhounds, the bassets, the beagles, the coonhounds, and the bloodhounds keep on keeping on. If they lose the line, they want to find it again.

Setters—all bird dogs—are also dedicated to their work. Today there are two types of Irish Setters, two types of English. You see one type, a bit smaller than the show dogs, far more at field trials. Most of you are accustomed to seeing these breeds at the bench shows. Many have never seen the hunting versions.

Mercifully, the progressive breeders and many judges recognized the damage being done by breeders who emphasize the "pretty" factor over other good, sensible traits. This has nearly ruined some animals for their original purpose. The worm is turning. I just pray it turns fast enough.

The Gordon Setter has rarely fallen victim to this dolorous practice, certainly not in the numbers that the Irish and English Setters have. Heavier than the other two setters, Gordons are good guard dogs and can hunt birds with the best of them, albeit at a different pace than the Irish or English.

Cocker spaniels really took a hit from reckless breeding, whereas field spaniels, Sussex spaniels, and the large Cumberland have remained intact, probably because they never caught the public's attention. I hope Stump's 2008 Westminster win doesn't change that. Sussex and Clumbers are an acquired taste, but once acquired, you can never live without one. I must confess that apart from my beloved foxhounds and my good bassets I am besotted with the setters and the field spaniels.

I have an Irish Setter, a big red female with wonderful bone and conformation. She guards the house and me. One of my neighbors learned this to his regret. He walked into the house without knocking and she bit him. Fortunately, he is a country man and realized he was at fault, not Tipper. But don't walk into my house if I'm not in it.

The hero of this chapter is a Gordon Setter. His prime showing days had vanished, if he ever had them, for he was blockier than he should have been. His coat gleamed and flowed. I do so love the Gordon coat. Well, I love Gordons in general. He walked through the hallways at the dog show, never raising a hackle or causing a problem. He caught my eye because I knew he didn't stand a tinker's chance in the ring. He exuded something. Yes, all Gordons do, but he seemed to have an extra dose of steel, that getting-down-to-business quality that I admire. The man walking him moved slowly and deliberately, pausing frequently to watch a class. Soon I was distracted from this Gordon as people I knew came up to chat, friends and acquaintances with their dogs on leads, a couple of judges on their way to the next class. AKC judges, like all of us, have partialities, but all are worth your time. The ones who can judge Best in Show are the top of the top. They are my rock stars, right up there with great huntsmen. By partialities, I mean each of them knows the breed standard forward and backward, yet there is wiggle room in every standard. One judge may like more bone in a Rhodesian Ridgeback than another, for instance.

The Gordon class filled one of the rings and I pushed my way over. At first I couldn't find "my" Gordon but then I spotted him standing quietly on the sidelines. Whew. I hated the thought of him being dismissed early.

Later, Skyline began offering a class for handlers. This was such a good idea. The focus was less about competition than about getting people in the ring with all manner of canines and helping them learn how to show under the eye of a good judge. The judge in this case was more than good. One kid, around twelve years old, give or take, was on the other end of a leash with a beagle, always a crowd pleaser. There was quite a crowd, too, since we all wanted to learn. In fact, you couldn't move. I was glad I'd hurried over early.

In walked my Gordon Setter. I, along with others, now really noticed his handler. I hadn't paid attention to the man during the show. I usually focus on the animal first rather than the owner. This middle-aged man had been damaged in some fashion. Whether he was born afflicted or this was the result of an accident, who knew? He moved a little off-kilter. His mind was not quick. However, he was correctly dressed and I perceived that no one was tending to him. He seemed to be self-sufficient and perfectly able to function. But it took him extra time to decipher a command.

The Gordon would sit when the judge called for that. The man would then stop as well. Each request from the judge was first obeyed by the dog. The human copied the dog. As the crowd began to understand what was happening you could hear a pin drop, to use the old expression. All eyes focused on this wonderful dog. When the judge asked for a little movement in the ring, what a show judge with horses could call a "trot," this majestic animal looked up at his owner, literally touched him with his front paw, and started to move out. The man did likewise but he struggled. In horse terms, he wasn't a good mover, which could have been the result of an accident. The judge, quite aware and so very kind, gave a little extra time. The others in the ring fell in step. This continued for twenty minutes.

When the class ended, the judge encouraged them all as he shook everyone's hand. The other handlers then went over and shook the hand of the Gordon's owner and petted the dog. Tears rolled down my face. I am not a crier and I loathe weeping in public, but I couldn't help it. Then I noticed just about everyone else was crying, too. Big men, small men, most of the women and the children. That man was so happy he glowed. The Gordon's tail signaled happiness, too. He looked up at the man and barked one note of joy.

Who of us would have the patience and the wisdom to work with a person like that? Some of you have these gifts and you are in professions where you do much good. I couldn't do it. Yet our dogs and many horses do it every day, and in the case of the Gordon, all day. Allied to the Gordon's love was the wisdom that his person needed extra time, extra care.

As always, dogs prove far more sensitive to human needs than most humans. Service dogs are miracle workers. They seem born with a wisdom we lack but we can learn.

My wish for each of us is that we find our own Gordon. None of us is as smart as we think we are. All of us could use some help. There is a dog out there, if you haven't found one already, that wants to make your life fuller. Give him or her the chance. You'll be a better person for it.

UG, short for Uninvited Guest. She brought an unusual message concerning an impending death. *Photo by Cindy Chandler.*

Stand and Fight

Mother taught me to fix the problem, not the blame. I try. I was also taught not to blather on about my personal life. One can discuss ideas, events, the all-important weather. What goes on behind your closed door stays there. Today I'm in the minority. Venting is a national pastime. It's supposed to be good for your health. Maybe it is, but it's not good for mine. A true friend can bring me any burden. I will share it. With a little luck and a lot of prayer, I might even be able to fix it. But with regard to the world at large, my feeling is essentially: shut up and get on with it.

Animals don't vent, whine, or collect injustices. They understand wrongdoing and punish it immediately. No lawyers. No remediation. No therapist. With a cat, it's a hiss or a whack across the snout. A dog will growl at a miscreant, and might try a takedown as well. Horse's hooves will fly, or their big teeth might remove a chunk of skin and flesh.

I see this over and over. If my foxhounds come in but one stays out, the others become upset. I'll look for the hound, as will hunt staff and club members who have worked with the hounds. Sometimes the laggard is young, not quite in the game. The older hounds might vocally abuse the youngster but no real harm is done when she is returned to the kennel. Their correction confirms my authority as head hound, as well as the fact that we hunt as a team, we return as a team.

Virginia, a noticeable girl with large dark brown markings on her glossy white coat, hunts like a demon. Every now and then, Virginia takes a notion. Tantalizing scent lingers here and there. She wants to pursue that scent whether I call her in or not. The other hounds know what she's doing.

When Virginia does come back to the kennel in her own good time, which happens often, one of us has to wait until the girls settle. When we put her in the "Big Girls' Run" the other hounds surround her and growl. If we don't step in, they will throw her down. If Virginia submits, she might endure puncture wounds on her hindquarters. If not, they'll tear her apart. Their sense of justice is strong. Virginia has done wrong. If I don't punish her, they will.

Do I punish her? No. I don't want her to fear coming back to me or to the kennels. So when she appears, in she goes. We let the bitching and moaning from the others run their course. Then a human, crop in hand, steps in and says harshly, "Leave it." That works a treat.

Without as many layers of so-called civilization, humans used to act more like hounds. People who didn't get along weren't harmed, but they were pointedly ignored. During times of severe repression (Cromwell's England, for example) an oddball might have been chastised in front of the congregation for not doing God's bidding with a happy heart. God's bidding, as I'm sure you know if you read history, mirrored whatever the Puritans wanted it to be. Selective reading of the Bible is hardly modern. You can justify anything this way.

Most humans don't believe that animals have a sense of justice or morality. "Morality" is a loaded word. Justice is easier to understand. Animals have a clear sense of justice. The punishment fits the crime. Once it did for us, too. If you stole something your hand was cut off, and so forth. Brutal? Yes. Also effective. Although I suppose you could learn to steal with the other hand.

Over the centuries, and especially in the last forty years, a sense of responsibility for one's actions has been erased. The damage that this disconnect from personal responsibility has done may be beyond calculation. Everyone living in America feels the effects but many don't want to deal with them.

Animals can't escape their responsibilities as we can. Their recourse is to kill or run away. Most choose the latter. If pack animals don't obey the pack rules, they are killed or driven to the edges. If they are killed, it's because they continually challenge the leaders. Humans still do this, too, but we cover it up better. Entire nations sit on the bones of murdered political foes. No nation has a clean record but some are better than others. Again, you can't judge the past by the present. People do, but how foolish.

If a hound can't get along in my pack, I remove it to a run where it stays alone, or with a few other hounds it does get along with. What's fascinating is that that same malcontent can still hunt well with the pack. It's the living together that doesn't work so well.

A dog will whine if it's upset or needs something, but no animal whines in the manner of a human. It's deeply boring when a woman does it and beyond the pale when a man does it. Patriarchy brings extra benefits, extra burdens. You want the benefits, accept the burdens. The problem with pushing down any segment of the population based on irrational criteria, e.g., color, gender, sexuality, is you must spend so much energy keeping an excluded group in its place. When the conquest is fresh, that energy takes the form of military or police. Over the centuries, elaborate ideologies were created to prove why the *untermenschen* are *untermenschen*. For some reason, this makes the top dog feel so much better about himself. The tragedy is that the oppressed so often internalize the definition of themselves as not as good as the top dog.

In real life a top dog in the kennels needs no such recourse. He or she is simply top dog—and often it is a bitch because the boys' minds wander, whereas the girls' minds focus like lasers. The top dog has earned his or her position through physical power and intelligence (there are no dumb top dogs) and willpower. Once every other dog or hound in the pack realizes the top dog will enforce her or his will, they fall in line. Calm ensues. Harmony reigns.

The horses behave in a similar manner. They aren't as quick to punish a horse who doesn't do what I ask, but, boy, will they nail one who doesn't do what *they* ask. What I notice about the horses is that if some are being naughty, the others distance themselves. When I walk into the paddock they look at me as if to say, "Jerks. Those boys are such jerks." If a horse is naughty to them, they usually kick him.

As a human, I don't always fathom the deep layers of responsibility, social interaction, and blood ties among humans. I try, but much is hidden and much is lost. What we are is a result of what happened many generations ago. A big moment, 1066. Not only did the English language change, the world changed. How could William the Conqueror know that his invasion gave those island peoples the last tool they needed to dominate the world? The dissolution of the monasteries during the reign of Henry VIII provided another great turning point. English-speaking people were cut off from Rome. If you didn't accept it, you were dead. It freed us intellectually.

Animals may have these turning points, but I expect they are evolutionary. As with us, much of the social or pack history is lost.

Even the physical package changes. Food is good; animals grow larger. Food is scarce, they shrink, become thin. More light and warmth, less hair. Each of us as an individual and as a member of our pack responds to the environment.

Humans believe they have a huge impact on nature. They do, but so do many other species, the beaver being an obvious example. The pine beetle or the boll weevil also changed the land. Every living thing leaves some mark, for good or for ill. The tricky part is that what's good in 1066 may not be good in 2010.

What remains constant are the great virtues of love, courage, compassion, and righteous action. Animals are capable of all of these virtues, as well as their opposites.

Some of you might balk at the idea of animals feeling compassion. If you sit in a chair and cry, doesn't your cat or dog come to comfort you? Mine do. I rarely cry but they know when I'm sad. Isn't that compassion? Once I came upon a dog that had been hit by a car. Its canine companion stayed there in the middle of the road to comfort its friend. No cellphone then so I put out flares (a good thing to keep on hand) and drove miles to a gas station. First I called the sheriff's department, since they'd respond the quickest to a potential car accident. As it was cold and rainy, the potential for an accident was real. That's why I set out the flares. An injured dog in the middle of the road could be dangerous for anyone driving on that road. Next I called Animal Control.

Those public servants did their job. The dogs were rescued. The hit dog didn't make it, but the rescuers did find the owner of the companion, who knew the owner of the deceased dog.

Compassion. Perhaps animals are further along than we are. A dog doesn't look at another dog and say, "I hate collies, I don't like their coats. They spend too much time with sheep, and they worship idols in the shape of collies." So I'd have to say they have more tolerance as well as compassion. They won't tolerate wrongdoing, but a dog, cat, or horse could care less if its buddy is chestnut, bay, gray, or pinto.

Each of my house dogs has a unique personality and a sense of independence. I encourage this, as long as it doesn't cause harm to the animal or to the rest of my household. Take Godzilla, the fat black-and-white Jack Russell. Sixteen years ago, she was given to me by my dear friend Joan Hamilton. Naturally everyone loved her. She considered it her due.

When Godzilla was eleven, Judy Pastore moved here from Los Angeles. After eight months of looking around, she found a house we all call "The Yellow Teacup" as it abuts my land, Tea-Time Farm.

Judy, being girly, transformed this place into one of great charm. Her pets have their own fenced-in yard with a big house in the back with tile floors. It's big enough for a person to inhabit. The dogs sleep in special beds, play with an abundance of toys, and just generally loll about in a canine paradise.

Godzilla has a habit of jumping into vehicles. People would visit me and a half hour after they left, I would receive a phone call. A strange noise alerted them while driving. The next thing they knew, Godzilla had leaped over the center console right into their laps. Usually I'd go pick her up. Sometimes, if the individual was a hunt club member, Godzilla would stay with them for two days, to be returned at the next hunt. In this way she acquired many treats. People thought the poor dear would be longing for home. The poor dear longed to be the center of attention. She was, and still is.

As Judy stayed here while working on her house, Godzilla would ride over with her for daily inspections. The little dog liked what she saw, recognizing this house as being quite superior to the one where she was currently quartered.

When Judy finally moved, Godzilla would again ride with her and even spend the night. One evening I couldn't find her. She had walked from my house to Judy's, a distance of perhaps a mile, some of it on the two-lane paved highway. She was returned the following morning, only to repeat her journey that evening.

My own dog dumped me.

You should see how she lives. I mean, I take good care of my dogs; I love them. They have toys, horses to play with, plenty of food. But they do not have a small palace to call their own. Godzilla has a special place in the palace, plus a special place in Judy's beautiful kitchen, a far cry from mine where only one burner works on the stove. I really do mean to buy a new one, but domestic needs take a far second place to farm needs, e.g., fencing, overseeing. I need a wife or a husband who can do such things. But given that my own dog left me, I know the chances of a human coming on board are next to nothing.

This dog is so spoiled, she even has her own wardrobe. Worse, she walks into my house and plops down so the other dogs see her. When she's had enough attention she leaves. Judy keeps her horses here, so Godzilla makes daily appearances. And appearances they are. Never have I met such a vain animal. Godzilla feels that every toy in my house is also hers. Thank God she can't get her paws on my checkbook.

As soon as she sails through my front door or enters via the dog door she comes and finds me, expecting lavish love. What's a mother to do?

Physical courage is obvious in any species. Emotional or intellectual courage—well, we know it when we see it but it's harder to pin down.

Physical courage often brings admiration, even rewards. Emotional and intellectual courage usually brings pain, since it often involves bucking the system. Decades or even centuries later, the individual may receive acclaim.

R.C., my large Doberman, may have had intellectual and emotional courage, but those qualities eluded me. Smart as he was, he couldn't read, nor did he involve himself in a complicated social life. Part of the house pack, the number-three dog, he knew his place and was content with it. My comings and goings fascinated him. Up he'd bound to sniff my shoes, then my pants legs. He stopped at my waist because I'd told him he needed to stay on the ground. Left to his own devices he would have stood on his back legs and been as tall as I am.

I always make sure Godzilla stays inside. R.C., being big, can face down the bobcat and bear that live here. Godzilla is too little. But even R.C. couldn't best a pack of coyotes.

About fifteen years ago we began to hear stories of coyotes being sighted in southwestern Virginia down near the Tennessee, North Carolina, and Kentucky borders where the states converge. By the early nineties, coyotes were sighted here.

R.C. and UG raised the alarm when coyotes would sneak here under the cloak of night. While a coyote can hunt alone, it prefers to hunt in a pack. If you see one when you're out walking, which I have, chances are you're surrounded. Unlike wolves, who could easily kill an unarmed human, they probably aren't going to attack you. Food is plentiful. There's no need. Also they're smaller than wolves. While hunting in a pack gives them an advantage, a human might be able to fend them off. Still, it's a good idea since the coyote invasion to carry a pistol or some other form of defense when walking alone, even in the daytime.

Coyotes in the East carry more weight than those in the West. They can run up to forty or fifty pounds if they're full grown. Living high on all our gophers, squirrels, house cats, chickens, newborn lambs and calves, they look like German Shepherds from a distance. Then you realize that they lack the shepherd's pronounced slope to the hindquarters and the noble Alsatian head. Curious, they'll often follow you, watching. Once when I walked out with the bassets and all the house dogs I saw a coyote sitting on a hill near my St. Thomas Equinus sign. He took a powder and the house dogs took off after him. Rudy, the Irish Terrier, remained behind. The Irish Setter, UG, and R.C. smoked right on that coyote's tail. By the time I reached the basset kennels, the house dogs had returned.

The bassets were excited by all the commotion as well as the scent. Coyote scent is heavier than fox, lighter then bear. Bassets hunt rabbits, an extremely light scent. They knew the coyote wasn't their quarry, but he smelled exciting.

My house dogs have a dog door, but if the coyotes are around I shut it at night to keep the cats and dogs in. Coyotes hunt at intervals around here; like most predators, they have a range, a schedule. A bear can hunt a one-hundred-mile radius. A coyote's radius is less. A fox's can be as much as twenty miles, but being the smart creatures that they are, they are usually a lot closer to the food supply. These radii appear in various game books. While the books are as accurate as human observation allows, animals don't read the books. Wide variation exists, which frustrates humans who want life, or foxes, to go by the book.

December 20, 2008, I let the dogs out. Tipper, the Irish Setter, went out with R.C. When the coyotes are on the prowl, I never let the dogs out alone. Tipper came back an hour and a half later. R.C. never came back.

The pack surrounded him and tore him apart. He took some with him. Courage. Some dogs, like some people, would have slunk down, hoping for a swift death. Makes sense. R.C. hoped for no such thing.

Had the coyotes attacked me, R.C. would have acted in the same fashion. A Doberman is born to protect and defend, and if you belong to one, he or she will die in the effort. I was sorry I wasn't with him, because we could have fought them off together.

Courage comes in all shapes and sizes. Small dogs will also die to defend you. Who would take on a Jack Russell? Not me. The fierce little dog could scoot right under the bellies of the coyotes. Then it would be a race for life.

Memories of R.C. stay with me. When the coyotes come for me in whatever form, be it human or illness or whatever launches me into the hereafter, I hope I have his courage.

My adored Esther, playing peek-a-boo. *Photo by Cindy Chandler.*

A Home Run

Most people recognize their duty in time to avoid it. Domesticated animals share this trait with us. While we all profit from having a job, there are times when we don't want to work.

Dad used to say, "You can make excuses or you can make money, but you can't do both." While I don't want to make excuses, there are days when I just want to play hooky. Don't you feel the same? But in my line of work, a deadline is a deadline. No manuscript, no paycheck. Same with the farm. Much as I might want to play baseball on a fine spring day, the fertilizer has to go down, the pastures need to be aerated. By the time you're finished, hitting that home run isn't even a daydream. It's twilight.

When I was small I'd watch the Percherons being turned out after a day at the plow. They'd rush into the pasture, kick up their heels, then settle down to groom one another or eat.

Cats, never touched by the gray brush of Puritanism, feel no compunction to be productive. They kill rodents because they enjoy it. Kittens' play mimics killing. For them, it's fun.

Much of animal play prepares them for the future. Human

play once did, too. Any game where hand-eye coordination is important is useful in hunting. Any game involving animals or music is also critical. Before telegraphs and telephones, people communicated with flames, smoke, and lanterns. But sound came even before that. Three key sounds produced by many European and Asian cultures were horns (originally animal horns), drums, and bells. The bells came later because we had to master metalwork first. Europeans and Africans brought their sound systems to North America.

Animal play involves sounds, too, but I'm not sure the purpose is the same. If two dogs are roughhousing and one cries "Uncle," the sound is high-pitched, short and sharp.

The rest of their play mimics hunting or herding. Stalking, bumping another dog to the ground, sitting on the downed dog, circling the dog, stealing one another's toys, and hoping to be chased—these are all mirrored in hunting or herding and reinforced by pack hierarchy.

Perhaps the most interesting form of animal play involves birds singing. Little birds in their nests or tree hollows listen to their parents sing. Some songs are territory calls, other are the latest news such as who is on the prowl. Songs vary. The little fuzzy things in their nests, mouths ever open, hear this. They hear us, too.

Scientists at the University of Chicago have recorded levels of activity in the brains of dozing birds. How they did this I don't know, but I read about it in *The Manchester Guardian* January 2–8, 2009. The small article explains that the sleeping birds had bursts of brain activity corresponding to what they had heard the day before. The babies were learning a new song. The scientists also played adult birdsongs to chicks. The next day, after a good night's sleep, the chicks sang better.

Maybe there's something to the practice of playing recordings of other languages (or even our own, since so few people master it these days) to your sleeping baby.

This isn't quite the same thing as true play, wherein you escape responsibility for a short time to engage in something that pleases you. But it does tell you something about the way creatures like to learn. Ever notice that if you're told you're going to learn something, you drag your feet? It's like being told to eat greens because they're good for you, not because they taste good. But if you're playing football with your dad as a lineman and he shows you how to upend someone's center of gravity, that's a good lesson. You've just learned how to flatten an opponent or human predator to get them out of the way. You've also acquired a little knowledge of physics.

Same with colors. Had my mother told me I needed to know about mixing red and yellow to produce orange, I would have listened politely but I might not have been interested. By simply doing it in front of me, she made it fascinating. Then she showed me how to breed flower colors. Even more interesting.

"Horseplay," like most Anglo-Saxon words in our language, reflects physical reality. Horses do play. They run at top speed, stop, and turn. That might throw off a predator, not that they know it at the time. Or two horses will stand on their hind legs to spar with each other, usually squealing for effect. If they lived in the wild this would mimic the younger stallion challenging the older. My advice to the younger stallion: Age and treachery always overcome youth and skill.

You probably play with your dogs and cats. With the dog you might play tug-of-war. They just love that. Some dog trainers will say that you must always wind up with the disputed object or you lose your dominance. I don't believe it. It's a game. Your dog knows it's a game. Let him win sometimes.

As for fetch, some dogs will bring back the ball, the Frisbee, or the sock you throw out until you're ready to drop from exhaustion. Some dogs prefer for you to throw the ball and you fetch it. They'd rather watch you exert yourself than do it themselves.

With a cat, bouncing a jack ball seems to bring delight. Many cats will retrieve, too. Any string you pull captures their attention. That game can go on for hours.

My favorite game with cats, dogs, and foxhounds is hide-and-seek. A very traditional English huntsman would probably frown on the games I play with my hounds. But I learned from those wonderful departed hounds born in the late 1930s and early 1940s that if I played with them, they were happy. They looked for me. If you're hunting hounds, you want them to look for you, to check back in. Thanks to playing hide-and-seek with the hounds I can hunt the old way, which is to say a loose cast. I can toss my hounds out there like marbles, knowing they'll roll back to me if I call.

Puppies learn so much when it's fun. What I like to do is to hide in one of the kennel runs (they're big, maybe a quarter-acre in some instances). They can't see me. Then one of my whippers-in, usually Emily Schilling, turns them loose, and I call for them. When they find me, it's cookie time. We'll do this in the summer once or twice a week. They love it. When I call them in during their first season hunting, they usually fly right back.

Games reinforce the fact that I'm the pack leader. Please me and wondrous events and goodies follow.

The same principles work with horses. There's a monster of

a jump. You can't see it, but your horse can. Eventually, without brutality, although you might have to get into him with the spurs, you take the jump. Usually you take it very, very big. You pat his neck, you tell him what a good boy he is. Always praise your horse. When you get back to the barn: cookies.

Never overwork an animal or a child. Short lessons produce better results than long ones. End the lesson with a victory.

It's either the carrot or the stick. I prefer the carrot. Play is one big carrot. Same with kids. There were no dishwashers when I was young, and I don't have one today. Just seems like a waste of electricity; but then I'm not feeding six. There were a lot of us at the table when I was young. We each had to take a turn washing dishes, including Dad. (Were my parents smart or what? Chores weren't assigned by gender. If they had been, our cars and tractors wouldn't have gotten fixed. Repairing vehicles was Mom's job, since she was good at it.) The repetitive chores rotated. Scrubbing off egg, hands in soapy dishwater, I hated it. But if I found a chipped cup or a chipped plate, I'd receive a nickel. I washed those dishes, glasses, and cups with an eagle eye. After the clean-up chores we'd sit down to play cards in winter. In the summer, when the light lingered, we kids would play kick-the-can. Then we'd come in and sit on the porch with the adults and play some kind of memory game or cards. Card games served as a backdrop for long chats about history, gossip, current events. You learned about your family, other people's families, what was in the news that day. I don't think that happens now since even the nuclear family is atomized. Kids don't know who their people are. No good can come from this. Okay, one woman's opinion.

Animals know who their people are, up to a point. A dachshund recognizes another dachshund, although I doubt the dog knows or cares about bloodlines. And species recognize one another as well as other species. Different species can play together. My cats and dogs play constantly. The big dogs flop on their sides and the cats attack. Then the dog gets up and chases them. The cat climbs onto the high back of a chair. The dog leaps into the seat. The cat jumps right on the dog, then off. The dog has to find the cat. Hide-and-seek.

One of the cats, Stonewall, grabs the Jack Russell, Tally, and rolls her over and over. Then Tally manages to stand up and pounce on the cat. But the cat, smarty, is on his back legs and claws out. The Jack Russell, being a Jack Russell, walks right into those claws, to be taken down one more time and rolled. What fun they have, and so do I.

Play brings us together, blows off steam. Wonderful though it is to learn through playing, it's pure joy to just let it all go.

Now if I could only teach them to play baseball.

Tack's story is one of great courage and heart. I miss her every single day.

Let Go of the Pain, Hold On to the Memory

C reativity is one percent inspiration, ninety-nine percent perspiration. That's not a bad formula for life in general.

When it comes to inspiration, there are many animals, people, and events that lift me up. I'm sure you have your own list. Mine includes Hannibal. What a brilliant military commander. Citation, one of the greatest Thoroughbred racehorses of all time. Pickett's Charge. What moves us also gives insight into our own character and that of others. People inspired by Pavlova might wish to be ballerinas, or they might be moved by her combination of athletic prowess and dramatic ability that great ballet stars possess. Others revere Teddy Roosevelt. God knows, he had energy. An engineer visiting Italy will surely be inspired by the aqueducts. And so it goes.

In my life, I've been fortunate to observe and study people with brains and grit. One without the other fails to impress me. Mother certainly had both. Dad, too, but what he gave me was insight into people, and emotional wisdom.

Three of the most inspirational people I have known were Countess Judith Gurky, Mrs. Paul Summers, Jr., and Virginia Moss.

Countess Gurky rescued her herd of Hungarian Warmblood horses during World War II. The Germans and the Russians rolled toward Hungary with the intention of strangling this remarkable nation, so different from the rest of Central Europe. Their language, flair, and superb horsemanship set Hungary apart. Hussars originated in Hungary. The Hussar is a form of light cavalry (soldiers who fight while mounted on horses, a form which has produced brilliant leaders like the American general Jeb Stuart).

Along the way Countess Gurky collected a Russian deserter, a German deserter, and an American lost from his unit. The four of them crossed the major rivers of Central Europe, were strafed, suffered, and lost a few horses, but not many. They made it to safety.

The Countess exhibited an imperious streak not uncommon in aristocrats born before World War I. She moved to southwestern Albemarle County in Virginia with her salvaged herd, which she managed to ship across the Atlantic. She had salvaged some resources, too, but like most people of her generation she experienced loss of land, country, possessions, money. She continued her great passion, and all of us who knew her, however slightly, felt her will, and her love for the horse. At the end of her days she dressed like a gypsy but you could still see the traces of beauty. John Western and Greg Schmidt, DVM, gave me an 8x10 photograph of the Countess, so beautiful, surrounded by her hounds. I prize it.

If one slender woman and three men at war with one another could perform this incredible service for animals, surely I can do my part.

Jill Summers's inspiring trajectory flew in a different direction. Growing up in Oxford, Mississippi, with an alcoholic father—William Faulkner—and a mother who endured but could drink a bit, too, her childhood created a wary, watchful, impeccably married Southern lady. The Faulkners had a child before Jill who had died. I'm not sure they hesitated to haunt her with that. At any rate, she was well acquainted with domestic pain. Not to say there weren't good moments in her childhood. She learned to love horses. She had the grace and generosity to care for her aged mother. She did not complain, she did not explain. Jill got on with her life. She never, ever traded on her father's name. She married a handsome, outgoing man, Paul Summers, Jr. Three children resulted. Like all children there were times when Jill and Paul could have just swatted them silly, but Jill was one of the best mothers I have ever known. Her love was unshakable.

Oh, the lady could ride. Like all fabulous riders she appeared to do nothing up there. She was Master of Foxhounds at Farmington Hunt Club for nearly forty years. Each year she bred a fine pack of hounds. That's a little like Joe DiMaggio's hitting streak but Jill did it every year. Without comment. Without drawing any attention to herself.

As most foxhunters hunt to ride, even those who had hunted with her for decades did not fully comprehend how extraordinary her achievement was. All the while, she was also a full-time wife, mother, incredible cook, and gardener. She could do anything except handle conflict. That's when she'd disappear. I expect she could handle it with Paul, as there's no such thing as a long marriage without sulphurous moments, or perhaps Paul figured out how to handle her.

Few people have experienced a childhood like Jill's, the fallout of worldwide fame (never to be desired, trust me on this) and the usual silly politicking inherent in subscription hunt clubs. A subscription pack is a miniature Congress. Enough said. My pack is a private pack, which means I am king. As Catherine de' Medici's son Charles of France once said, "It's good to be king." Sure hope I'm a better one than he was. Although Charles IX (1550–1574) did write *Traité de la chasse royal*.

Another human I have admired tremendously is Virginia Moss, MFH of Moore County Hounds in Southern Pines. Like Jill, she could ride. She bred lovely Thoroughbreds. Expansive, warm, hospitable, she gladly gave of her knowledge, her refrigerator's contents, anything. When I first met her she was in her seventies, sailing over four-foot fences, some larger as they'd been poached out in front, without a bobble. Slim, smartly turned out, she'd smile at a member and their confidence would soar. Ginny transmitted courage as well as goodness. I wouldn't be where I am today with my hunt club if it hadn't been for the years that sweet soul indulged me. Twice a year I'd drive down to Southern Pines to visit with her and hunt with Moore County.

The other glorious thing about Ginny was she could be funny without being malicious. She was around ninety-five when she left us. If you knew her, you'd agree, that was too soon. We need another ninety years! She had so much left. I cherish everything she gave to me.

When I started my foxhunting mystery series, I rolled up parts of Jill and Ginny and threw in the magic of invention. In Sister Jane Arnold there is also some wish fulfillment on my part. She rides better than I do, and she's a far, far better Field Master than I was when I filled that position. For one thing, I'd bedevil my huntsman too much, and for another, people in my field kept falling off, which was more my fault than theirs. I'm a better huntsman.

Those who read the Sister Jane series fall in love with her. She's an inspiration. The one trait I share with Sister Jane is that we're both determined. We have grit.

But humans aside, the most inspirational creature I have ever known, who still guides me today, was a Belgian Shepherd Greendale, a black beauty with a hint of flat-coat retriever tossed in.

I found her in the middle of a country dirt road not far from my farm in Nelson County. She'd been run over and was screaming. She was only about six weeks old. I picked her up, which hurt her, but I spoke to her low and she calmed down. I drove to the closest vet (Dr. May wasn't in Nellysford yet so I had to get into Waynes-boro). Many of her bones had been broken. She was so small it would have been very difficult to set them. The vet, a young lady, was so kind. She asked if I wanted to put the little thing down. I looked into this puppy's sweet brown eyes and said, "No, I'll take care of her."

The vet suggested that when she had grown perhaps we could rebreak her bones and set them correctly, providing that she lived.

She lived. She slept by my bed. I carried her around. Her bones knit quickly and I put her on every bone-enhancing supplement, every oxidizer I could find. There she'd be, in my lap, opening her little mouth as I'd pop in a bit of a pill, smothered in butter. She was too young to swallow whole ones. In six weeks' time she had healed. Everything healed crooked. One shoulder popped up higher than the other. Her forelegs had two big lumps where the bones had broken but they weren't too terrible. Her hips and hind legs were crooked. She couldn't have cared less. That was the hap-piest dog I have ever known, the most courageous.

At the risk of bragging, Tack worshipped me. And I her. She never tried to bite me when in pain. She wagged her tail every time she saw me. She loved riding in the truck. When fully grown, she'd come along to exercise the horses. Three sets a day adds up to six miles. She'd lope along regardless of the weather. Cold weather had to settle in her bones, because it does in mine. Not a peep. Only bright eyes and eagerness. She ate anything you chose to give her with ladylike delicacy and gratitude. Her whole life was gratitude.

Friends who could ride would sometimes do a set with me, including Dana Flaherty, my forever professional whipper-in. Sometimes these friends would ask with concern, "Isn't that dog in pain?"

Would I allow an animal in pain to do this six days a week? She wasn't in pain. She developed beautiful muscles that helped support her. Her coat shone like anthracite. She'd sometimes talk when she ran, out of sheer happiness.

At age twelve she creaked a little when she'd rise in the morning. Time for Rimadyl. By age fourteen the arthritis was pronounced, but she still wanted to go out on every set. We allowed her one a day because those two-mile runs were good for her circulatory system and her muscles. And she'd go once her Rimadyl kicked in.

Close to fifteen, her movements slowed and her hearing was compromised a little. No more sets. I'd shout "Walkies!" and she'd hustle to the front door for a leisurely mile walk, just the two of us. She smiled the whole time.

One warm day, I hopped into my nice Volvo station wagon. My friend Judy Pastore was in the driveway on foot and we were chatting by the driver's window. I had the wagon in reverse and drifted back, under five miles an hour, but I bumped into Tack who was back there waiting for me to drop the door. She wanted her ride. She let out a scream.

Judy ran back to her. Tack lay on her side. I joined Judy and we lifted her up. She flopped down. Distraught but not losing it, I put my hands under her belly, straddling her while Judy slowly walked in front and we led her into the house.

We found an old blanket and Tack gratefully lay down. She ate well, drank. But her motor skills eroded. Then she couldn't control her bladder.

She'd only been knocked over. A football tackle hits far harder. Nonetheless, I felt terrible over what I'd done to this marvelous dog.

After four days of lifting her in and out of the house, holding her up (she weighed about seventy pounds), it became obvious that Tack wasn't going to bounce back. The arthritis, age, her original injuries, and my last insult had done their work.

I called Anne Bonda. She drove the forty-five minutes from her clinic to help us. Judy and I put Tack in the bedroom, because she wanted to sleep near me as she had all her life. Anne brought her assistant, Joanne. Tack lifted her head. She was alert but slipping away. I petted her and told her what a great dog she was. Then Judy ushered me out. Anne gave her her shot. Tack left us. Well, Anne cried, Judy cried, Joanne cried, and I tried not to, without much success.

Tack touched everyone who knew her because of her great courage, joy of life, and devotion.

I know she forgave me that bump. The lower tailgate of the Volvo is metal, and with her lying down just ready to get in the back, I couldn't see her, and neither could Judy.

I couldn't forgive myself. I mourned my dog and cursed myself for months. I couldn't think about her without a knot in my stomach and tears in my eyes. Not in front of anyone.

Then one day I thought, "Tack loved me. Maybe she loved me more than any human or animal in my entire life. She wouldn't want me to be miserable. She'd want me to be happy, and to help other dogs, cats, and horses." That's an obvious pep talk but it felt like truth to me.

I let the pain go.

Now what I remember best is her courage, her love, her desire for my striped socks. Why the striped ones and not the white, I will never know.

I hope I can be as courageous as Tack. I hope you can, too.

Rev. Judy Parrish blesses the animals before a hunt.
Photo by Danielle A. Durkin.

Gimme That Old-Time Religion

The last part of 2008 and the first few weeks of 2009 witnessed some of the largest temperature swings ever recorded in the Mid-Atlantic. I've never seen anything like it. January 18, the mercury read minus 2 degrees Fahrenheit at 5:30 A.M. The cold remained bitter for days, then an ice storm sent us beauty and broken bones. After that, the mercury started bouncing. You'd wake up and it would be seventeen degrees. By noon it would be forty-five. The next day you'd wake up and it would be twenty-four degrees; by noon it would be sixty-two. Just about everyone I know, including myself, hosted a virulent respiratory bug complete with fevers, chills, and a racking dry cough. It felt like you-know-what. For some people this lasted two full months. Luckily I sweated and shook for two days, then pulled out of it. Well, not quite, as I was still coughing. Voice faded out, too.

Seneca said, "Scorn pain. Either it goes or you do." I live by that. I did, however, not attend mass at St. John in the Woods, a beautiful chapel Patricia Kluge built. She invited some of us to attend mass held by Father Gregory. He gives you much to consider, and in a way that brings out the best of you, none of these fear messages.

Missing mass is one thing. It was easy to make that decision as I didn't want to be close to people and risk giving them the bug. Not taking out hounds is another. They needed to go, and people have paid money to belong to Oak Ridge Hounds. Plus I could do it without getting close to people so I felt it was safe. I went out, even on bitter days, with not much by way of padding since my fever kept me warm.

February 8 we met at Cherry Hill, an estate built just before the Revolutionary War. Simple, not gaudy, and so lovely, people flock to hunts at Cherry Hill. The owner, Miss Anne Henderson, welcomes us each time, always acting as though we are doing her a favor by hunting her land when it is quite the reverse.

Not for the fainthearted, Cherry Hill tests hounds, horses, and riders. The land around the house undulates, then quickly rises to the top of Turner Ridge, perhaps twelve hundred feet above the highest pasture. From the ridge you can look down and see the Upper James River, pastures hugging its banks, still in winter garb. Now that the bald eagles are back, you occasionally see them, too. In fact, you might see them at any of our fixtures north of the James. So far, we've sighted none south of the James.

Trying to suppress my cough, I threw my leg over Dodger, a sixteen-hand Thoroughbred/Oldenburg cross. I'm not a big warm-blood fan but I do understand why other people are, and Dodger has taken the best of both. Marion Thorne, MFH of Genesee Valley, hunted him with a broken collarbone using one hand. Marion's tough. Dodger's kind. I'm in love with him. He's still making up his mind about me, although after yesterday I may have won his heart.

When we started at ten A.M., it was already fifty-seven degrees. It had been cold that morning (another big temperature bounce), which kills scent. It was the day before a full moon, a promising omen as all animal activity peaks around the full moon, but those that rushed out too early could now be sound asleep in their dens. You can't get a fox up the day after a full moon: too much partying.

Hounds cast on the north side of Cherry Hill, moving through Anne's herd of Angus cattle like the pros they are. A little feathering (tail-wagging) but no one spoke. I told the field it would be a quiet day. I lied, but I didn't know it at the time. If you read the books, this should have been a zip day, and the last two weeks sure were. Hey, I'm not complaining. At least we went out. Many hunts were idle for two weeks because the snow and ice would start to melt, then freeze up during the bitter night. The next day would be worse.

Dodger and I popped over a log jump, not really big, maybe three foot two if that. Hounds had opened. Hooray, at last! We were on Judge Whitehead's land. The judge and his pretty wife, Sandra, allow us to hunt this chunk except during deer season. Foxes like it there, so we usually get something going. Did the fox use the lovely trail our members had cut for him? No. He ran up the hill through the nastiest stuff. My face felt the thorns, one found its way into my ear. The ones in your nose really sting. Anything that sticks out can stab you. But hey, you have to follow the fox. Right when we got into the worst of it, he vanished. Great. Now what? Orion, one of the best hounds I have ever hunted behind, a draft from Deep Run (thank you, thank you, Deep Run) came back to me and looked up. "Well? What do you want me to do?"

I told him to stick with me, blew the three long notes that mean "Come to me." Wiggling through underbrush came the rest of the pack, down some, since most of the girls were in season, plus the hounds with high metabolisms can go out only once a week. They run off too much fat if you take them out more than that. It's cruel to take a hound out that doesn't have enough fat to keep him warm.

The only way out, and it wasn't inviting, was up. It's not too steep but it's thick. Dear Dodger kept his head down and pushed through. Behind me I was receiving blessings from the field. It was Sunday. Hey, the fox took us there. It was not my idea.

We finally pushed out into the cemetery of the tidy Bethel Brethren Church. Dodger had never been to church before so his ears swiveled. Maple, Cheerful, Orion, Zachary, and the others stopped in their tracks. The pack that had visited Trinity Episcopal are mostly gone now, as that was over a decade ago. Plus, an Episcopalian service differs markedly from a Brethren and the few hounds that were on that adventure are now retirees working with puppies, so there was no made hound who could say "Keep going."

Inside it was that old-time religion. The hounds wanted to join in. I couldn't blow the horn and disturb the service, so I kept whispering, "Pack-in to me. Pack-in to me."

With the help of Emily Schilling, honorary whipper-in, and Karen Osborne, whipper-in in training (which means neither of them gets paid for one of the hardest jobs in foxhunting), we managed to convince the hounds not to attend the service. The door was closed, which helped. Years ago the vestibule door had been open at Trinity. Ever see a pack of hounds filling up a church vestibule? Impressive.

We crossed Variety Mills Road and Emily hopped down to open the gate. Bet we'll be putting a jump in that fence line in the future.

Willie was missing. Karen Osborne returned to the churchyard. A lady was visiting a grave. Willie sat with her. Karen dismounted and quietly called him. He came, then returned to the lady. Finally, the lady took him by the collar and walked him to Karen.

Karen apologized, but the lady, obviously a dog lover, said she liked the company.

Karen Osborne walked him back to the other side of the road.

Willie smiled. Most of our members recognize him because of his big smile. He made the lady smile, too.

You have to love Willie.

"That's it," I thought to myself, once we were all together. "It's in the mid-sixties. I'm sweating bullets and I know my fever's gone. We aren't going to do squat."

But the field was ready. Many of them wore trophies of what we'd fought through: twigs, pine needles, thorns. Everyone had risen between four and five-thirty in the morning for this. The hounds were ready. The worst that could happen was that we'd enjoy a ride in stunning weather.

For an hour I was right. We crossed a creek; the coop (a jump like a chicken coop) sat in water, lots of water. Fortunately the gate was open. Since I'm huntsman, I usually take the jump first unless a whipper-in has preceded me for some reason. But when you have water or deep mud, each horse that takes the jump deepens the hole, so to speak. We call it "poaching out." No one minded missing that jump.

A cool air current always swirls down at a low spot. Didn't do us any good. The hounds worked steadily. Up at the sunken farm road, Orion, at the top, paused as I dipped down to cross the creek again. I called. He kept his nose to the ground.

Trust your hounds.

He opened. All the hounds flew to him.

The chances of getting a run on a day like this are about the same as being hit by a meteorite.

"Watch out below. One's coming."

They all opened and shot straight up, parallel to the creek that tumbles amid boulders and large rocks down from Turner's Ridge.

We went straight up too. Dodger comes from territory with deep non-red clay, some very good soil as well, and some deep ditches, not exactly ravines but you need to ride down them and then ride back up. They are too wide to jump. This was new to him, I think, but he's a trouper. Up and up we climbed, finding creative ways around the narrow path where saplings had fallen in the ice storm.

The hounds sounded great.

At one point, I lost the last part of the trail up. The rains and ice had obscured our path. We had to move around the large rocks churned up thanks to the glacier.

We forged a new path. Dodger was breathing a bit hard, but not as bad as he might have been because he's kept in good condition. He's a strong horse, too.

I looked down to view the field as hounds slowed for a moment. In particular, I noticed two lovely people who were in their second year with Oak Ridge. Since I'm forward I rarely have the opportunity to turn around and see how the field rides. Mary Jane and Tom Timmerman were up in their stirrups right over their horses' center of gravity, which makes it easier on the horse. You'd think both would be grimacing, worrying about the climb, the narrowness. Big grins. A few other members were smiling, too. This sort of climb separates the sheep from the goats, literally.

Four years ago we had visitors, flatlanders. The fox ran the same pattern and a goodly number of them suffered the vapors. Bob Satterfield, not yet a joint MFH, kindly gave up his day hunting to turn them around (not easy), walking them back to the trailers where a stiff drink revived them.

I don't think it's so bad, really, but I'm used to it.

A pause, some air, then Cheerful and Maple opened again with Orion right there. The fox ran just below the top of the ridge on the western slope. We followed on the ridge. He criss-crossed over and back twice, then thought better of it and headed down on the Upper James River side. I called the hounds back. They came. We walked and slid down on the western side on a better path since we'd already traveled quite a bit.

Once in the high meadow we sat and caught our wind. I had a couple and a half up there and called them down. They did return after we'd moved off.

I may have told you, you always count hounds in couples. Been doing it that way since the Pharaohs, and if it ain't broke, don't fix it.

The hounds tried some more but the mercury now registered seventy-one. My truck has a thermometer, and once we were back I checked it.

Hounds, horses, and humans shared a wonderful day. Everyone's spirits were high, and some of our members had not had an easy time of it lately. Two of them had undergone serious operations; one, still at home, received the full report via telephone. The other one, John Loughlin, with his wife, a doctor who could have been a runway model, came on foot. Nothing can dim John's spirits, but the recounting of that day made him giddier than usual. Other members have lost their entire portfolios. We don't have many people with lots of money, but even someone with money doesn't want to lose it. Some of our members worry about keeping their jobs, since so many firms are letting people go and small businesses are shutting down.

That great day gave everyone a respite, reminded them what's really important: health, companionship, nature's beauty.

Lifted me right up. Didn't even mind my cough.

Nature abounds in beauty. Just look at this great blue heron. Smashing!
Image courtesy of Alan D. Wilson, NaturesPicsOnline.com.

Birds of a Feather

A great blue heron, male, fishes at my small pond. His mate sometimes joins him, and when little herons hatch and begin to fish, they're down there, too. Twice a year, a female bald eagle also shows up. She causes a ruckus. Since the eagle and the heron eat the same foods, they dislike each other. The blue heron has an extensive vocabulary that flies like shrapnel. The cackle is loud. I can hear it when I'm pulling weeds behind my stone wall.

The eagle rarely responds. Eventually the heron closes that long bill and gigs frogs. If you've ever been physically near either of these birds you will admire them. The great blue male, if he stretches to his full height, is taller than I am at five foot four. He's not afraid of me. I can often draw within forty yards. If I stay still he allows me to watch him fish. His quickness as he uncoils that long neck startles me. We pay millions of dollars to male humans if they have good reflexes for certain sports. Compared to this guy, we're all painfully slow.

The eagle's eyesight astonishes. All birds have marvelous eyes, but I read somewhere that an eagle two miles up can spot a mouse moving on the ground. I don't doubt it. She won't allow me as close as the heron but she's not afraid of me. Her talons terrify. My face could be shredded in an instant. Fortunately, eagles disdain human flesh, as do many animals. We can be thankful that we don't taste good. If you've ever visited countries whose standards of hygiene fall below our own, you begin to understand why most animals want nothing to do with us. Humans stink. Odd to say, if a tiger or lion does kill humans and eat them, they develop a taste for it.

There's an old saw: The bird that sits is easily shot. In the nineteenth century, a rage for feathered hats gripped Europe and the Americas. The heron survived even though its feathers are lovely. Today no one shoots herons. Why would anyone wish to do so? They are so beautiful. Same with cranes. They reflect peace and calm. To me, anyway.

The eagle, on the other hand, like all raptors, represents power, predatory prowess. Nations reveal their innermost drives by their totems. Ours is an eagle. That imperial symbol served Rome well. Remember when Caesar Augustus would occasionally fall into his cups and cry for Varus's lost eagles? The Germans wiped out Roman legions stationed at Coblenz. It is an extraordinary story that all of us who learned Latin read if we got beyond Virgil. *National Geographic,* that most excellent magazine, has covered this beautifully, in words and photographs. What a thrilling piece of detective work.

Long and short: we have always wanted to be a great power, even in the beginning when we were weak. Ben Franklin thought our symbol should be a native bird, the turkey. In a backhand way, Ben got his wish. Congress is full of them.

Life on this farm finds no one day like any other. Right now the birds are mating. Calls fill the air. The male sings out; if the female's interested, she answers. Otherwise, a depressing silence follows. The ground nesters do "the dance." Watching them reminds me how exhausting it is to find a mate. I know I've said this before, but the exhaustion falls on the male.

Another month will go by before mares go into season. The foxes are mating, which means we enjoy our best runs chasing a visiting dog fox. Two years ago during February I picked up a dog fox. He gave us a merry chase for twenty hard minutes, then popped into the den of another fox. That fox, whom I know (he's still there and fat as a damn tick), happened to be resting, maybe reading Anthony Trollope's marvelous works on foxhunting. You should have heard the fuss. The air was blue. However, by this time all the hounds surrounded the den. When hounds put a fox to ground, they sing, dig, and are so excited. But they can't dig out the fox, as the dens are cleverly built. Another fox who lives on my farm has many exits and entrances, one right over a creek bed. I've heard him leave his abode by that exit, flopping right into the water.

While my pack has put many a fox to ground, they never heard anything like this cussing and swearing. No one moved. Suddenly the two arguing gentlemen realized a pack of foxhounds stood at the door. Silence. They patched up their differences, at least until the hounds left.

Skunks are traveling today, too. Give them wide berth. House dogs never seem to learn this lesson, so during mating season I go through a lot of tomato juice, lemon juice, and Skin-so-Soft, which, mixed together, somewhat diminishes the odor. Lots of rinsings help, too.

Then there's eau de possum. A possum inhabits my attic. There's no getting her out, which means there will be more possums. I will sometimes see her moving out at night for gleanings. Ugly as a mud fence, they are dear animals.

I usually go to bed by nine, read until ten, and get up at 5:30 A.M. in winter, 4:45 to 5:00 A.M. in summer. I rise about 1:30 A.M., read a little more, then go back to sleep. I've always done this, as did Mother. The night envelops one. That's when I see my waddling possum. If I have them, I put out marshmallows near her entrance. She gets a treat coming home near dawn.

Squirrels in the attic present more commotion than the possums, who are quiet and respectful. The squirrels run around, thump, thump, thump. Rude, too. If I sit under the oak tree that they use as a launching pad, they chatter. If the cats join me, they throw acorns. A well-tossed acorn smarts. The cats, outraged, climb the trees. More acorns. The squirrels then leap to the roof and slither under the eave. The cats leap to the roof, too, but can't reach the squirrels.

Deer, raccoon, bobcat. My bears (whom I like, but from a distance), all the hawks, kestrels, and kites, the indigo buntings and bluebirds, all the animals are perking up. Even though it's winter, they know before we do when spring is arriving. Given the breeding patterns, this will be a normal spring: not too late. Based on their carryings-on, I figure the crocuses will be up in mid-March. After that it's a progression of color, beauty, tremendous excitement. The winter birds return, including certain breeds of hawk who use the thermal spirals to rest on their way to New England and Canada.

Spring fever grips all of us. The horses get silly. The cats are always silly, only more so. The dogs evade my calls to come in but finally comply. The symphony of life will hit the first movement. Mid-March is the overture.

Do you come down with spring fever? I do. I'll rise extra early so my daily pages are knocked out by the second hour of sunlight. Then it's out the door, not to return until sundown. For one thing, I like to visit the different hunt fixtures (the farthest is two hours away) to put out higher protein food for my. foxes. I don't want the vixen to have to travel far to eat. She rewards me, come hunt season in the fall, with bracing runs. I know many of my foxes, and most know me, too. It's a pleasant arrangement.

A gardener's shadow is the best manure. Time to start digging. The finches, robins, bluejays (they'll fly right down and look up at you, they are so bold) watch intently as I stir up grubs and insect goodies. When the praying mantis pods open and those tiny green babies pop out, the birds really are in heaven. It's amazing any survive, but many do, and by September these huge praying mantises hang on everything. They eat the bad bugs, so I'm not complaining, but it gives you a shiver if one flies to sit on you.

Our bee population has diminished. This is a tremendous worry, bigger than the economy. If the bee dies, we die. It's that stark and simple. As two of our hunt members are deathly allergic to bees, I have not put out bee boxes, although I'd like to. For whatever reason, bees will sit on me and not sting. Butterflies sit on me as well. Since butterflies also adore sitting on horse manure, this may not be flattering. As for the bees, I take it as a compliment. I have loved them since childhood, since Mother explained to me that all human life depends on bees.

The ticks and chiggers emerge, too. Hateful. What does God need with chiggers? I have bemoaned this all my life with no answer forthcoming. Better a wasp sting you than chiggers get you. The scars last for months.

I mentioned the economy. As you read this, we'll most likely be at the bottom of this worldwide depression euphemistically called anything but. The Great Hypocrite, Gordon Brown, points the finger at the United States, ignoring the fact that his Labour Party is equally responsible. London is the world center of finance, even more than New York. As the world castigates us—much of it deserved—why do they look to us to pull them out? Well, if the eagle is our totem, we'd better start flying.

Here's a partial answer, and it is provided by animals. Forget old capital. It's lost. Create new capital. When a skunk has a litter and one dies, she may mourn but she turns her attention to the living. We should do likewise.

We're at a turning point. If we lead the world, then we must lead in reconstituting our relationship to vital resources, in developing new industries and technologies. I'm willing to bet that many innovations formerly disregarded will now be revitalized. And some will be just miraculous. If we don't do this, billions will die. Not millions—billions. It may not be our responsibility to save the world—our first responsibility is to save ourselves—but if there's any left over, we should share.

And we must rethink our relationship with our sentient creatures. Let them be. Better yet, learn from them. Basic survival concepts: Don't breed past the food supply. Always, always protect the female. Don't waste.

Few animals waste. A dog may overeat; a horse certainly will if you forget to close the feed room door. They'll kill themselves on food provided by humans. It's not that they're stupid. Watch them eat in a natural setting: they put their heads down, pull up sweet grass, chew, move on. It takes a lot of pulling and chewing to fill that big stomach. But if the food is right there in front of them they don't know to stop.

Stupid? Well, how stupid is it for humans to eat so much fat when living in cities? Fat is to keep you warm. I eat far more fat than is recommended. There are days when I'll eat three thousand

calories and I'm small, weighing between 125 and 128 pounds.
I can't keep the weight on. But I live outside. I work hard physically. I burn calories like the Great Chicago Fire. I need the fat.
Many Americans with less active lifestyles don't need so much fat,
hence the obesity epidemic.

Animals rarely commit the mistakes we do, which is one of
the main points of this book. If we respect them, observe, and
learn from them, we will commit fewer mistakes.

Nature's mistakes die. Cruel but effective. We have a mania to
preserve life, even if that life cannot be lived without terrible suffering and pain. It should be the individual's decision (and this
will upset some of you). We prolong agony, exhaust cash reserves.
Wouldn't the wiser course be to encourage a life to be well lived?
Allow people dignity, and that also means the dignity to die. Suicide upsets me to my core, but if someone is dying and refuses
their medicine, I don't think that's suicide. I've seen my hounds,
dogs, cats, and horses make that decision. God willing, I will
know when to make it for myself, barring an accident that will
hasten me out toward life's red exit light.

What animals have taught me is wisdom, deep wisdom.

Chaser, an Orange County hound drafted to me as a puppy
by Adrian Smith, then the huntsman there (he's now at Deep
Run), taught me about dignity. As I mentioned before, my experience with the Orange County C line is that mentally they take
an extra year to mature. Many huntsmen think they're stupid and
draft them out. The Master might say, "Get rid of that hound. He
isn't going to amount to a hill of beans." If the huntsman knows
the line's history, the hound will be drafted to some other lucky
hunt.

Adrian gave me Chaser because he had so many puppies that
year and he kindly remembered I liked the C line. (There isn't a

bad Orange County line, just like there isn't a bad Deep Run one, either. You can't miss.) Well, he was ungainly, slow. Year one he learned his name and came to the horn. Of course, I didn't hunt him. I knew better. Most of my hounds of Orange County blood are slender and elegant. Not Chaser. But that voice! Deep, resonant, clear, and majestic, truly majestic. Verdi would have loved him. By year two, I allowed him to hunt at the fixture that includes my farm. His attention did not wander, though he was often puzzled. By year three he was matchless. Steady, determined, and very patient, he would find the line and sing out in his basso profundo.

Once over at Oak Ridge (a miracle in itself), Chaser, although not terribly fast, had gotten ahead of the pack, all of whom were milling about a pool of scent perhaps three hundred yards off. He came up on a thicket where a deer and her tiny fawn hunkered down. He stopped cold. He sniffed. He looked up at me. I didn't want to bolt the deer. I hadn't known they were there, as they were so well hidden, but Chaser could tell. I can smell deer in rut but I could not smell the mother and fawn. Human noses are so frustrating. Deer will run to live, but the fawn looked still wet to me. I couldn't take the chance.

I shook my head at Chaser and put my finger to my lips. He knew finger to lips and he walked over to me. We reversed the hunt in the opposite direction. A good day, too, for we flushed out one of Oak Ridge's famous black foxes. How beautiful they are, and how clever. Once this one tired of the chase he jumped from cow patty to cow patty, then took off to pop into his den which is (still) under a large rock across the railroad tracks.

Chaser won my heart. I love all my hounds but some stand out. Strong—I could hunt him twice a week. A few times, if the ground was tight as a tick or there was ice, he became footsore. He'd sit down and lift a paw, and on would go the bag balm. He'd follow me around in the large boys' run. Not particularly talkative, he liked to be close. Sometimes I'd take him out for a special walk. You can't do this often: if you single a hound out for special treatment, the others become jealous. If you aren't careful you can set up terrible kennel fights. I would take along other hounds, too, who needed some exercise due to muscle strain or whatever. If I'd sit down on the kennel flower box, he'd sit at my feet. If I allowed him into the tiny office, he'd lean on my leg as I sat in the chair. We'd sit side by side discussing our thoughts on how to improve the pack. Ours was the physical rapport of deep friendship.

Years passed swiftly. Chaser got some age on him, so John and I included him in hunts only once a week. I lived to hear that sonorous voice, so recognizable that even people in the field knew it. This is no slur on the field. Few foxhunters can identify the different hound voices, whereas as Master I need to do so. It's like hearing your children. A mother usually knows which one is speaking even if everyone is yelling at once. Where you run into difficulty is that often a hound will sound like one of his parents. But that's not so bad, because that hound often hunts like one of his parents, too.

A big, powerful hound, when he neared his tenth birthday, Chaser began to thin down. The oldest foxhound I had, Tassel, made it to sixteen. Her last years verged on spoiled luxury as she flopped on Bob and Sue Satterfield's rugs. That was a happy, happy girl.

Chaser didn't want to leave the pack. He hunted the rest of that year. During the summer he walked out with the puppies, providing leadership. For the youngsters, walking out with the pack of hounds is a big step up. The first few times it might over-whelm them. Chaser would be coupled to one and the kid's confidence would rise. Didn't take long for that youngster to walk without a mentor.

More time whirled away and we put Chaser in his own special run. No one wanted to see him get bumped by another hound. He'd been a power in the pack and that's how he should be remembered—with dignity. He deserved his dignity. I'd walk him alone; no need to worry about jealousy now. John fed him extra rations. He hung in there, tail wagging, happy with life.

My wonderful editor at Ballantine, Judy Sternlight, visited. She met Chaser, who behaved like the Virginia gentleman that he was. He impressed her. When she'd call, she'd always inquire about the big boy. Judy was so taken with Chaser that he gave her the idea for this book. I wouldn't have thought of it. Three cheers for Chaser and Miss Judy!

I should explain, I am published by two houses, both under the Random House umbrella. Judy Sternlight is one of my editors; the other is Danielle Perez at Bantam, another animal lover.

One day, Chaser looked up with those large warm eyes. He'd started into renal failure. It wasn't bad yet, and I was going to make sure it never reached that point. We talked. The kennel's interior bunk is long so we could sit side by side, pressed close. We said our goodbyes. He left this earth with love and gratitude and he kept his dignity.

Chaser loved me and I him. He was kind to other creatures, even during the occasional insufferable cat visits to the kennels. My former whipper-in, Dana, lived across from the kennels and one of her cats, Maybelline, is a real pisser. No other word for it. Maybelline would sashay down to the kennels and sit outside the chain link fencing to inform the hounds what she thinks of them and dogs in general. It is not complimentary.

Behind the kennels, a Manhattan of fox dens covers the earth. Hidden in the undergrowth and pines, those reds come and go. At night they, too, will sit outside the kennels. Sometimes the hounds announce their presence. Other times I swear they swap stories. I'll find fox scat all around the kennels.

Chaser knew these foxes. When we'd hit one—not often, because they'd recognize hunt kit and go home (very unsporting)—anyway, on the odd occasion when we'd pick one up, Chaser would sing and sing. Then he'd go to the den and sit down. No point digging. He knew that. He could be so funny about it.

So here I sit. The Blue Ridge Mountains, those ancient sentinels to time, face me. Behind me, Ennis Mountain offers a hint at the glaciers' power. Some of the boulders at the top of the ridges look as though a stonemason smoothed their sides. They're beautiful, and also full of foxes.

These mountains, once the tallest in the world, now soft and caressed by time, threw up the first barrier to westward expansion. I can see, far away on the other side of the Shenandoah Valley, an Allegheny peak, another barrier that stretches all the way to Charleston, West Virginia—of course, it was all part of Virginia until the War Between the States. Once past Charleston you approach the Ohio Valley, a source of such rich soil.

The Blue Ridge separates Celtic and English ways from German ways, for the Valley is very German. On this side there is a tacit recognition that people are no better than they should be, that life is theater, so play your part. On that side, they tend to be more serious. If they stray from the straight and narrow, I think they carry more guilt. A few of us here might carry some, too, but mostly we figure to be human is to make a mess. The point is: Is it an interesting mess? The worst sin we can commit is to be boring. Small chance of it, I declare.

People ask me, "Where do you get the ideas for your stories?" All I have to do is look around or plumb my family or anyone else's family history. What an inexhaustible vein of pure, pure gold.

While people give me the ideas, animals give me the energy. I draw sustenance from them, perspective, wisdom, and such loyalty. By their loyalty they put ours to shame. Mostly, I live on the love.

Lately I have been entertaining the idea that God might not be an American. Allied to this is the suspicion that this Great Spirit doesn't resemble us at all. To say we are made in God's image is outrageous human vanity. But if it truly is the case, then man was the experiment; woman, the perfection. Poor old Adam and his rib!

Animals eschew stories like that. Their spiritual dimension is deeper. We used to embrace this back when we worshipped the twelve Olympians and the various demigods. The American Indian—I just can't say Native American, it sounds like an insurance company—still believes.

As an aside, the people changing these designations like undergarments usually are doing so for some political gain or to siphon money out of Washington. Someone told me you can't use "Native American"; now it has to be "First American." The first American was a protozoan.

Whatever you call them, when you think of the sheer guts of those people who took on the army even when they saw the technology we possessed, the only word that is appropriate is "warrior." Those who don't understand how they could ride to their deaths have neither honor nor heart nor animal courage.

Unfortunately, that covers so many now. Animals certainly have courage. As to honor, I believe it. Chaser had honor. My beautiful Diane had it in spades. A cat may have honor but it's not quite the same. Some humans will scoff at these ideas should they ever pick up this book. I can't help them. They are not as smart as they think they are, and in good time, life will make this abundantly clear.

As to heart: whatever the species, we recognize this. As we trod across the rubble of many civilizations, what pulled us through? Heart. No matter how intelligent, if you don't have heart you won't work for your salvation or anyone else's.

The core American experience is loneliness. A New World. Vast spaces. Miles and miles before coming upon another human, whether of European, African, or Warrior descent. Sometimes days, months. It's deep in our character.

But alone as one might have been back then, there was probably a dog walking with you and your horse, should you have been fortunate enough to own one. Cats killed the mice even if you lived in a sod hut. We never were truly alone.

And neither are you.

I hope you are lifted by the love of a cat, dog, horse, even a parrot like Mother Brown's Franklin. More, I hope you recognize it and return it. I pray, and I mean pray, that you will send a few dollars to your local SPCA to help those that have been abandoned, some mistreated.

We are all in this life together. We need one another.

I hope that those animals and people I missed—creatures who were in need—will forgive me. I'll try to forgive myself. It's vanity not to, because it implies that I should be better than anyone else. I'm not. I hope my dear horses out in the pastures and my house full of rescues will be patient with me and continue to guide me. I'll do my best and I think you will, too.

Remember: we left Eden, they didn't.

Photo by Danielle A. Durkin.

Acknowledgments

Special thanks to Judy Sternlight, who on visiting the farm was so taken with Chaser, one of the foxhounds, she suggested this book. She was a dream to work with and loves animals, too.

PHOTO: DANIELLE A. DURKIN

RITA MAE BROWN is the bestselling author of the Sister Jane novels—*Outfoxed, Hotspur, Full Cry, The Hunt Ball, The Hounds and the Fury, The Tell-Tale Horse,* and *Hounded to Death*—as well as the Sneaky Pie Brown mysteries and *Rubyfruit Jungle, In Her Day, Six of One,* and *The Sand Castle,* among many others. Emmy-nominated screenwriter and a poet, Brown lives in Afton, Virginia.

www.ritamaebrown.com